AF173755

Palgrave Frontiers in Philosophy of Religion

Series Editors
Yujin Nagasawa
Department of Philosophy
University of Birmingham
Birmingham, UK

Erik J. Wielenberg
Department of Philosophy
DePauw University
Greencastle, IN, USA

Palgrave Frontiers in Philosophy of Religion is a long overdue series which will provide a unique platform for the advancement of research in this area. Each book in the series aims to progress a debate in the philosophy of religion by (i) offering a novel argument to establish a strikingly original thesis, or (ii) approaching an ongoing dispute from a radically new point of view. Each title in the series contributes to this aim by utilising recent developments in empirical sciences or cutting-edge research in foundational areas of philosophy (such as metaphysics, epistemology and ethics).

Alberto Oya

The Metaphysical Anthropology of Julián Marías

palgrave
macmillan

Alberto Oya
IFILNOVA
Universidade Nova de Lisboa
LISBOA, Portugal

ISSN 2634-6176   ISSN 2634-6184   (electronic)
Palgrave Frontiers in Philosophy of Religion
ISBN 978-3-031-61803-1   ISBN 978-3-031-61804-8   (eBook)
https://doi.org/10.1007/978-3-031-61804-8

© The Editor(s) (if applicable) and The Author(s), under exclusive license to Springer Nature Switzerland AG 2024
This work is subject to copyright. All rights are solely and exclusively licensed by the Publisher, whether the whole or part of the material is concerned, specifically the rights of translation, reprinting, reuse of illustrations, recitation, broadcasting, reproduction on microfilms or in any other physical way, and transmission or information storage and retrieval, electronic adaptation, computer software, or by similar or dissimilar methodology now known or hereafter developed.
The use of general descriptive names, registered names, trademarks, service marks, etc. in this publication does not imply, even in the absence of a specific statement, that such names are exempt from the relevant protective laws and regulations and therefore free for general use.
The publisher, the authors and the editors are safe to assume that the advice and information in this book are believed to be true and accurate at the date of publication. Neither the publisher nor the authors or the editors give a warranty, expressed or implied, with respect to the material contained herein or for any errors or omissions that may have been made. The publisher remains neutral with regard to jurisdictional claims in published maps and institutional affiliations.

This Palgrave Macmillan imprint is published by the registered company Springer Nature Switzerland AG.
The registered company address is: Gewerbestrasse 11, 6330 Cham, Switzerland

Paper in this product is recyclable.

¡Adentro!

Preface

My decision to write this book evinces my conviction that Marías's position is philosophically interesting in itself and deserving of serious and rigorous analysis. My writing it in English rather than Spanish, my (and Marías's) mother tongue, reflects my conviction that Marías's position should be made accessible to an international philosophical audience. I hope this book promotes further discussion on Marías's works, and above all that it somehow contributes to the philosophical task of reaching a better understanding of ourselves, and thereby of God.

Platja d'Aro   Alberto Oya
20 de enero de 2024

Contents

About the Author

Alberto Oya (PhD) is *Investigador Doutorado Contratado* at the Instituto de Filosofia da Nova (Universidade Nova de Lisboa, Portugal). Oya has published over 30 papers in professional philosophical peer-reviewed journals, and he is the author of the books *First-Person Shooter Videogames* (Brill, 2023) and *Unamuno's Religious Fictionalism* (Palgrave Macmillan, 2020).

1

Introduction

Abstract This brief introductory chapter outlines the structure of the book.

Keywords Christianity • Death • Hope • Jesus Christ • Julián Marías • Metaphysical Anthropology • Personal immortality • Resurrection • Revelation • Salvation • Introduction

This book provides a detailed account of Julián Marías's Metaphysical Anthropology with the ultimate aim of offering a coherent and systematic analysis of Marías's argumentation for claiming that my (each one's) conscious hope for Christian Salvation through Resurrection—and with it my hope that Jesus Christ did actually resurrect, and more generally my hope for Christian Revelation to be true—is justified not because I am justified in affirming the truth or the likelihood that this Salvation will actually occur, but because this hope of mine is a legitimate reaction on my part, inasmuch as it amounts to a self-affirming exercise, a conscious endorsement of my own (each one's) *human* reality, and as such a sign of authenticity.

© The Author(s), under exclusive license to Springer Nature Switzerland AG 2024
A. Oya, *The Metaphysical Anthropology of Julián Marías*, Palgrave Frontiers in Philosophy of Religion, https://doi.org/10.1007/978-3-031-61804-8_1

The book is divided into seven chapters. The aim of the chapters that follow on from this first introductory chapter can be briefly outlined as follows. Chapter 2 is a biographical introduction to Julián Marías. Chapter 3 offers a detailed account of Marías's Metaphysical Anthropology. Marías's Metaphysical Anthropology expands in an innovative and philosophically relevant way on José Ortega y Gasset's ontological claim that *my life* (each one's) is the *radical reality*, which is why Chap. 3 begins with a detailed analysis of Ortega's argument for making this claim. Chapter 4 discusses Marías's argumentation for claiming that *my life* (each one's) presupposes, not as an epistemic attitude of part of I myself, the executive I, but as an ontological postulate intrinsic to *my life* without which *my life* itself as *radical reality* is *impossible*, the assumption of its own indefinite perduration. Chapter 5 analyses Marías's argumentation for concluding that my (each one's) conscious hope for Christian Salvation through Resurrection is justified as it being a conscious endorsement of my own *human* reality, inasmuch as only if the Christian God were to exist and save us through Resurrection would be the ontological postulate intrinsic to *my life* (each one's) regarding its own indefinite perdurance be satisfied. Chapter 6 contrasts Marías's position with that of Miguel de Unamuno, thereby helping to better situate Marías within the framework of the history of Spanish Philosophy. The last concluding chapter overviews the analysis offered in this book.

2

Biographical Introduction: Julián Marías (1914–2005)

Abstract This chapter is a biographical introduction to Julián Marías (1914–2005). An outline of Marías's life is given, and his most well-known essays and philosophical works are pointed out.

Keywords Biography • Julián Marías • Life and works

Julián Marías Aguilera (known as Julián Marías) was born in Valladolid in 1914 and died in Madrid in 2005 at the age of 91. Throughout his long life, he was an extremely prolific writer in terms of both volume and range of topics. Among his writings we find not just what may be labelled as strictly speaking philosophical books and academic papers, but also newspaper and magazine articles, anthologies, travel literature, translations into Spanish of classical thinkers such as Seneca, Aristotle and Leibniz, and edited texts with annotated commentaries.[1] Marías also authored a long and beautifully written memoirs, originally published in three separate volumes during the years 1988 and 1989, and later

---

[1] A list of Marías's published books and essays can be found in Roldán Sarmiento (2007).

© The Author(s), under exclusive license to Springer Nature Switzerland AG 2024
A. Oya, *The Metaphysical Anthropology of Julián Marías*, Palgrave Frontiers in Philosophy of Religion, https://doi.org/10.1007/978-3-031-61804-8_2

compiled on a single book entitled *Una vida presente* (Marías 1988–1989) [*A Present Life*]. In his memoirs, loyal to his philosophical conviction that a *human life* can only be apprehended narratively, he tells his own life story in an effort to show himself as a person and not as just an author.

Marías's passion for cinema serves to illustrate both his wide range of interests and his extremely prolific writing activity. In 1956, he wrote the essay *La imagen de la vida humana* (Marías 1956a) [*The Image of Human Life*], in which he argued that cinema allows spectators to experiment with different paths of acting—which he named as "trajectories" ("*trayectorías*") in his philosophical essays—in a way that is more profound than other form of fictions such as theatre plays and novels allow for. To this effect, his writings on cinema far outweighed any other topic in terms of volume. Following *La imagen de la vida humana*, which may be considered a theoretical essay, came the publication of over 1000 articles in which he commented on the aspects of specific films which, for one reason or another, caught his attention.[2]

Given the large number of writings Marías produced and their thematic diversity, it is outside the scope of this biographical note to exhaustively analyse all and each one of his works—and a mere enumeration would fail to do justice to their content. My aim in this chapter is not, therefore, to analyse in depth each and every one of Marías's writings but rather to offer readers an outline of his life while pointing out his philosophical works that are most relevant for the philosophical claims discussed in this book. Fortunately, with the sole exception of *La felicidad humana* (Marías 1987a) [*The Human Happiness*], all the relevant works in this regard have already been translated into English and so are easily accessible to an international academic audience.[3]

As will become evident in what follows, Marías's life was deeply interwoven with the two major political events in Spain's recent history, the

---

[2] Most of these articles were published in the journals *Gaceta ilustrada* (with which Marías collaborated between 1962 and 1982) and *Blanco y negro* (with which Marías collaborated between 1988 and 1997). A complete list of these articles is available in (Basallo n.d.). Some of them have been compiled in *El cine de Julián Marías. Volumen I. Escritos sobre cine (1960–1965)* (Marías 1994) [*The Cinema of Julián Marías. Volume I. Writings on Cinema (1960–1965)*] and in the two-volume work *Visto y no visto* (Marías 1970a *and* 1970b) [*Seen and Not Seen*].

[3] Despite not having been translated into English, *La felicidad humana* is available in Portuguese (Marías 1987b) and Italian translations (Marías 1987c).

Spanish Civil War (1936–1939) and the consolidation of a democratic system in the late 1970s in the form of a constitutional monarchy. To this effect, and without pretending to be an exhaustive scholarly historical analysis, this chapter also aims to give non-Spanish readers a first glimpse into the admittedly complex political situation of twentieth-century Spain.

As already mentioned, Marías was born in 1914 in Valladolid, a city located in the northern centre of the Iberian Peninsula, in the Spanish region of Castilla y León. In 1919, his family moved to Madrid, in the centre of the Iberian Peninsula, which was then and still is the capital of Spain. In 1931, at the age of seventeen, Marías began a degree in Philosophy at the University of Madrid, where he was a student of Manuel García Morente (1886–1942), Xavier Zubiri (1898–1983), José Gaos (1900–1969) and, most notably, José Ortega y Gasset (1883–1955). At university, Marías initiated a long and sentient friendship with one of his classmates, Dolores ("Lolita") Franco (1912–1977), who later became his wife and the mother of his five sons. Marías was an excellent student, obtaining his bachelor's degree in June 1936 and planning to begin his doctoral studies under the supervision of Xavier Zubiri after the summer break, in September 1936. However, and unfortunately, on July 18th the *coup d'état* that began the Spanish Civil War took place.

Some Spanish territories supported the *coup d'état* while others remained loyal to the established Republican government. Not only the military but also the political parties, trade unions and individual citizens took sides. From thereafter, and until May 1939, Spain was divided into a two-sided military confrontation between the Republicans and the insurgents, who self-proclaimed as "*los nacionales*" ("the nationals"). The insurgent movement, at first led by a military directorate, soon acquired a fascist and authoritarian tone. From October 1936 onwards, all power became ultimately concentrated in General Francisco Franco (1892–1975), proclaimed by those on his side as "*Generalísimo*"—the superlative form of "General", so its literal English translation is "the most General". For its part, the Republican side was soon dominated by the anarchist, socialist and communist factions, who arguably seemed more interested in taking advantage of the instability of the moment to achieve a "social revolution" than in defending the constitutional order of the Republic. Moreover, each of the factions understood "social revolution" in its own particular way, leading not only to political tensions but on occasion to violent armed clashes within and between the Republican side. Also worthy of mention is the different relationship the two sides had with religion. While the insurgent movement proclaimed themselves as defenders of Catholicism, even to the point of declaring their side as a "*Cruzada por Dios y por España*" ("Crusade for God and for Spain"), most of the areas under the Republican control, with the important exception of the Basque Country, suffered varying degrees of anti-clericalism, which included not only the closure of places of worship, but also violent persecutions against clergy and lay Catholics.

Marías stayed in Madrid, which remained under the control of the Republican government until the end of the war. He was called to arms by the government, in fact serving as a translator. Profoundly Catholic throughout his life, and defining himself as "republican" and "liberal", he remained loyal to the Republican side throughout the war—even though, as previously mentioned, the Republic at that time had little about it that was either liberal or Catholic. In his memoirs, Marías bases his support for the Republican side on his stance against the war, bearing in mind that it was the insurgents who, in the first instance, had incited it:

> There is one thing that should be kept in mind and it is decisive if you want to understand something. Once in a state of war, that is, *given the war*, upon this supposition, it was very difficult, if not impossible, to not take part in it. *Preferring* one of the two factions was unavoidable, which does not mean to approve of it or be complicit in it. One could believe that one or the other side was more right than the other, or that it was less dangerous, or more capable of correction and rectification. That is why it seemed to me, even back then, that one could be in good faith on one or the other side, as long as one was, first of all, *against the war*. "Within" it, there could be different reasons for one or other option. Mine was in favour of the Republic, firstly because the rupture of concord had not proceeded from it, because the aggressors had been the insurgents. Yes, it will be said, but with reasons. Certainly, but they were not reasons enough, not reasons enough to start a war. In favour of the Republic, but from a critical stance, with energetic reservations, with immense repugnance for the acts that were committed in its name; and with the evidence that similar things were

being done on the other side of the trenches. From the first moment, the only thing that seemed desirable to me was the *end* of the war. And my support went, first, to those who had neither wanted nor caused the war; second, to those who felt its pain; third, to those who wished or intended to finish it. (Marías 1988–1989, pp. 145–146, author's emphasis; see also: Marías 1988–1989, p. 155)[4]

While Marías did not go into battle, he did play a relevant role at the end of the Spanish Civil War. Once Catalonia had been taken by the insurgent troops at the beginning of 1939, most of Spain was under the control of the insurgent side—Madrid and Valencia were the two only major cities remaining under the control of the Republican government. On 27th February 1939, France and the United Kingdom recognised the insurgent side, led by General Francisco Franco, as Spain's legitimate government. The next day, Manuel Azaña (1880–1940) resigned from his position as President of the Republic and went into exile in France. By that time it was obvious that the Republican side had lost the war. Nonetheless, the Republican government, now presided over by Juan Negrín (1892–1956), was not willing to capitulate.

Given the situation, and to avoid mounting a resistance that would not only have been ineffective but would have brought the country more death and destruction, some Republican leaders organised a *coup d'état* to overthrow the Republican government and form a new temporary

---

[4] My translation. The original Spanish text reads: "Hay algo que conviene tener presente, y que es decisivo si se quiere entender algo. Una vez en estado de guerra, es decir, *dada la guerra*, sobre supuesto, era muy difícil, si no imposible, no participar en ella. Era ineludible *preferir* una de las dos fracciones, lo cual no quiere decir aprobarla ni ser cómplice de ella. Se podía creer que uno u otro bando tenía más razón que el otro, o que era menos peligroso, o más capaz de corrección y rectificación. Por eso me pareció, ya entonces, que se podía estar de buena fe de un lado o de otro, con tal de que se estuviera, en primer lugar, *contra la guerra*. 'Dentro' de ella, podía haber motivos para una u otra opción. La mía fue a favor de la República, en primer lugar porque la ruptura de la concordia no había procedido de ella, porque los agresores habían sido los sublevados. Sí, se dirá, pero con motivos. Ciertamente, pero no suficientes, no como para hacer una guerra. A favor de la República, pero de una manera crítica, con enérgicas restricciones, con inmensa repugnancia a mucho de lo que se hacía en su nombre; y con la evidencia de que al otro lado de las trincheras se hacían cosas equivalentes. Desde el primer momento, lo único que me parecía deseable era el *final* de la guerra. Y mi adhesión iba, en primer lugar, a los que no la habían querido ni provocado; en segundo lugar, a los que sentían su dolor; en tercer lugar, a los que deseaban o se proponían terminarla".

directorate with the exclusive aim of achieving a peace treaty with the insurgents. The *coup d'état* of 5th March 1939 was led by Coronel Segismundo Casado (1893–1968) and it established in Madrid the *Consejo Nacional de Defensa* ("National Defense Council"), made up of anarchists, left-wing republicans and moderate socialists, but without the support of the communists, who rebelled against its authority. There were violent military clashes with the communist troops led by Coronel Luis Barceló (1896–1939) and the rest of the republican military troops within the city of Madrid, which went in until March 12.

One of the central figures of the *Consejo Nacional de Defensa* was Julián Besteiro (1870–1940), member of the Spanish Socialist Party and someone Marías already knew as a Professor of Logic at the University of Madrid. Marías did not become a member of the *Consejo Nacional de Defensa*, and was not expected to take part in the hoped-for peace negotiations—which eventually did not take place because Franco rejected all attempts at dialogue and would only accept unconditional surrender. However, Marías did play his part in spreading the mission of the *Consejo Nacional de Defensa* by conveying to the population the reality of the situation—that the war was now over and not only coexistence but "*convivencia*" among all Spaniards needed to be restored.[5] At Besteiro's request, Marías wrote several articles, some of which were published in the Republican edition of the newspaper *ABC* and others broadcast on the radio. According to Marías, he wrote these articles with the aim of liberating people on both sides of the war from the purely propaganda

---

[5] The Spanish term "*convivencia*" is usually translated into English as "coexistence". However, this term fails to capture a slightly but nonetheless relevant meaning of the term "*convivencia*", which is distinguished from "*coexistencia*" in Spanish. "*Convivencia*", unlike "*coexistencia*", is not just existing together but living together. Marías himself is explicit as to why "*convivencia*" should not be equated with "coexistence": "And this Spanish word ['*convivencia*'] seems precious to me: in many languages it does not exist, but is substituted by the word '*coexistencia*', which is a very different thing. Coexist means everything that exists together and at the same time. Things coexist, and man with them; '*convivir*' is living together, and it refers to persons as such. That is, with their differences, with their discrepancies, with their conflicts, with their struggles within '*convivencia*', of that operation that consists of living together" (Marías 2000, p. 11). My translation. The original Spanish text reads: "Y esta palabra española ['convivencia'] me parece preciosa: en muchas lenguas no existe, y la sustituye la voz 'coexistencia', que es cosa muy distinta. Coexiste todo lo que existe juntamente y a la vez. Las cosas coexisten, y el hombre con ellas; convivir es vivir juntos, y se refiere a las personas como tales. Es decir, con sus diferencias, con sus discrepancias, con sus conflictos, con sus luchas dentro de la convivencia, de esa operación que consiste en vivir juntos".

statements they had previously been receiving, and with the ultimate intention of favouring "*convivencia*" among all Spaniards:

> For peace to be made in Spain—and I am not talking about the negotiations with the other side, which were totally outside my reach and which *were not the decisive thing*—the first thing that was needed was the expression and dissemination of the truth. It was necessary to blow away the thick cloud of lies that had enveloped all Spaniards in both zones since the beginning of the war, so in this way they could install themselves into reality. It was necessary for the Republicans to understand and accept their defeat and recognise the extent to which they had contributed to it with their errors and their crimes; and the adversaries also had to see the part they had played in the same evils, even if luck—perhaps undeservedly— had been on their side. It was not enough to talk to the inhabitants of the Republican zone because peace, if it should come to that, was a matter for both of them. So all Spaniards had to be addressed at the same time, saying the *same thing* to them both. It could not be anything but the strict, and certainly painful truth. And it had to be done in a way that was heard and not rebuffed; that could be accepted and have its effect of leading towards a spirit that would make peace possible. (Marías 1988–1989, pp. 180–181, author's emphasis)[6]

On 27th March 1939, the *Consejo Nacional de Defensa* commanded the dismantling of the defence of Madrid by the Republican troops. The insurgent troops entered Madrid the next day, and on 1st April 1939 Franco officially declared victory and the end of the war. The Franco dictatorship had begun with Franco himself officially proclaimed as "*Caudillo*

---

[6] My translation. The original Spanish text reads: "Para que se pudiera hacer la paz en España –y no me refiero a las negociaciones con el otro bando, que estaban totalmente fuera de mi alcance y que *no eran lo decisivo*–, lo primero que hacía falta era la expresión y difusión de la verdad. Era menester barrer la espesa nube de mentiras que envolvía a todos los españoles de ambas zonas desde el comienzo de la guerra, de manera que se instalaran en la realidad. Era menester que los republicanos comprendieran y aceptaran su derrota, y reconocieran en qué medida habían contribuido a ella con sus errores y sus crímenes; y que los adversarios vieran también la parte que tenían en los mismos males, aunque la suerte –acaso inmerecida– los hubiera acompañado. No bastaba con hablar a los habitantes de la zona republicana, porque la paz, si llegaba a ser eso, era asunto de las dos. Por tanto, había que dirigirse a todos los españoles a la vez, diciéndoles *lo mismo*. No podía ser más que la verdad estricta, y ciertamente dolorosa. Y había de hacerlo de manera que fuera escuchada, no rechazada; que pudiera ser aceptada y hacer su efecto de llevar hacia un espíritu que hiciera posible la paz".

de España por la Gracia de Dios" ("*Caudillo* of Spain by the Grace of God").[7] He was president of the Government of Spain until 1973, and head of state until his death in 1975.

Shortly after the war ended, Marías was arrested and spent a brief period in prison. Due to his serving as a translator for the Republican side and his already mentioned collaboration with the *Consejo Nacional de Defensa*, he was excluded from the official intellectual institutions of the Francoist regime and was thereby impeded from obtaining a faculty position in Spain. There is an event in Marías life that clearly illustrates this exclusion while also reflecting the intellectual poverty of Spanish universities at that time and the tight control the Francoist regime exercised over them. After the war, Marías renewed his intention to write a doctoral dissertation under the direction of Xavier Zubiri, completing it and defending it in January 1942. However, the thesis committee, made up of supporters of the Francoist regime, failed it without giving a clear academic reason as to why. The sole exception on the committee was Manuel García Morente, who firmly opposed this decision. Marías's dissertation was, however, published as a monograph under the title *La filosofía del Padre Gatry* (Marías 1941b) [*Gatry's Philosophy* (Marías 1941a)], achieving a wide circulation. As Marías pointed out in his memoirs, the fact that it was published meant that "[e]verybody could read it and judge it—and judge its judges" (Marías 1988–1989, p. 239).[8]

Despite his uneasy situation, Marías resolutely decided not to abnegate his philosophical vocation. He simply accepted that, given the circumstance he happened to coexist with, he "[…] would have to work harder and live more modestly" (Marías 1952, p. 496).[9] Marías decided to put his greatest effort into writing books. These books would not only have to be philosophically substantial enough to satisfy his own philosophical vocation, but have to be attractive enough to as many people as needed

---

[7] The Spanish term "*caudillo*" can be translated into English as "leader" or "chief" and can be considered as the Spanish equivalent of the Italian "*Duce*" and the German "*Führer*".

[8] My translation. The original Spanish text reads: "Todo el mundo pudo leerla y juzgarla –y a sus juzgadores".

[9] My translation. The original Spanish text reads: "[…] habrá que trabajar más y vivir con más modestia".

to guarantee sufficient sales to be able to make a living. With this in mind, Marías wrote *Historia de la filosofía* (Marías 1941d) [*History of Philosophy* (Marías 1941c)], which was more successful than he initially anticipated, its first edition of 3,500 copies rapidly selling out (Marías 1988–1989, p. 225). It was in this period, and fruit of his interest in the philosophy of Miguel de Unamuno (1864–1936), that Marías also wrote the book *Miguel de Unamuno* (Marías 1943b [Marías 1943a]), which is one of the earlier (if not the earliest) serious monographical studies on the philosophy of Unamuno. In 1947, he published *Introducción a la filosofía* (Marías 1947b) [*Reason and Life: The Introduction to Philosophy* (Marías 1947a)], which can be considered as Marías first attempt to offer a systematic philosophy of his own.

In 1948, Marías published *Filosofía española actual (Unamuno, Ortega, Morente, Zubiri)* (Marías 1948) [*Present Spanish Philosophy (Unamuno, Ortega, Morente, Zubiri)*]. An enlarged edition that included Marías's essay "Presencia y ausencia del existencialismo en España" (Marías 1950b) ["Presence and Absence of Existentialism in Spain" (Marías 1950a)], was published in 1959 under the title *La escuela de Madrid* (Marías 1959) [*The School of Madrid*]. This book is relevant to mention here in that there he declares himself to be a disciple not only of José Ortega y Gasset but also of Miguel de Unamuno, Manuel García Morente, Xavier Zubiri and José Gaos (Marías 1948, p. 9; Marías 1959, p. 223). The book contributed to the use of the expression "*Escuela de Madrid*" ("School of Madrid"), a term which is now used to refer to the Spanish philosophers of the twentieth century whose philosophical views were somehow influenced by Ortega—including, among others, the already mentioned García Morente, Zubiri, Gaos and, of course, Marías. The term "*Escuela de Madrid*" serves to distinguish these authors from the kind of scholastic philosophy that was officially taught in Spanish universities in the forties and fifties. The term "*Escuela de Madrid*" has also been used in contrast to the "*Escuela de Barcelona*" ("School of Barcelona"), with the aim of distinguishing two allegedly distinct intellectual traditions in twentieth-century Spanish philosophy. The term "*Escuela de Barcelona*" is used to refer to the philosophers who were somehow related to the University of

Barcelona in the 1930s, including Jaume Serra Húnter (1878–1943), Joaquim Xirau (1895–1946), Eduardo Nicol (1907–1990), Joan Roura-Parella (1897–1983) and Josep Ferrater Mora (1912–1991). However, aside from the more political than philosophical intention of emphasising the geographical origin of these authors as the Spanish region of Catalonia, and the fact that some of them wrote some (not all) of their works in Catalan, the distinction has little real meaning in that most of the authors that are now commonly ascribed to the *Escuela de Barcelona* were already influenced in one way or another by Ortega's works. Consider, for example, Joaquim Xirau, who may be regarded as the most prominent philosophical figure of the so-called *Escuela de Barcelona*. While not endorsing Ortega's philosophy, Xirau shared Ortega's concern of overcoming the philosophical dispute between idealism and realism (see: Oya 2022).

Marías's relationship with Ortega intensified after the latter's return to Spain in 1945. They were now no longer just teacher and disciple, but they were also great friends. Strictly speaking, Ortega was not prosecuted by the Francoist regime, but he was blocked from resuming his position as Professor of Metaphysics at the University of Madrid. Moreover, even though he already enjoyed of considerable international recognition, and many considered him as the most important Spanish intellectual alive at the time, those in charge of the university were eager to delegitimise him and bury his legacy. According to Marías, there was even a conscious and systematic attempt on the part of some Spanish Jesuits to force the inclusion of Ortega's works in the Catholic *Index Librorum Prohibitorum* ("Index of Forbidden Books") (Marías 1988–1989, p. 283). At the time and until 1966 when the *Index* was formally abolished by Pope Paul VI (1897–1978; Papacy: 1963–1978), Catholics were not allowed to read the books included in the *Index* without previous explicit ecclesiastical authorisation. In response to this plan, Marías wrote his essay *Ortega y tres antípodas: un ejemplo de intriga intelectual* (Marías 1950c) [*Ortega and Three Antipodes: An Example of Intellectual Intrigue*], which was published in Argentina to avoid the Francoist censorship. These Jesuits did not succeed in their endeavour and none of Ortega's books was condemned by the Catholic Church.[10]

In 1948, both fully aware that they had no place in the Spanish university system, Ortega and Marías co-founded in Madrid the *Instituto de Humanidades* ("Institute of Humanities"). It was conceived as a private educational institution where courses and conferences would be held, not only on Philosophy but also on the Humanities in a broader sense (see: Instituto de Humanidades 1948). However, the *Instituto de Humanidades* did not enjoy of great success and in 1950 it ceased its activities. The lack of success was largely due to the fact that even though the Francoist regime did not overtly prohibit or censor its activities, it did restrict their dissemination and advertising.

In 1951, coinciding with the appointment of a new Dean at the University of Madrid, Marías at last obtained his PhD, receiving the highest qualification of "excellent"—and this with the very same doctoral dissertation that nine years earlier had received a fail for no clear reason. Obtaining the academic title of PhD did not mean greater opportunity for Marías to enter the Spanish university system. It did, however, prove useful for Marías's activity in foreign universities, which would begin the very same year, 1951. As Marías explains in his memoirs: "The doctorate particularly helped me in foreign countries, so that I did not have to explain why I did not have it" (Marías 1988–1989, p. 285).[11]

Throughout the 1950s and 1960s, Marías's international impact grew steadily, and he began to regularly give lectures and courses at different universities and educational institutions in the United States, Latin America and Europe. In 1951, Marías was invited to spend a year as a visiting professor at Wellesley College in the United States. While there, he was invited to give two courses at Harvard University in the summer

---

[10] It should be emphasised that not all Spanish Jesuits were of the opinion that Ortega's works should be condemned as libellous to the Catholic creed—as Marías puts it: "I must say that the book [*Ortega y tres antípodas: un ejemplo de intriga intelectual*] earned me the friendship of several Jesuits, who were grateful for the fact that I had pointed out something they were ashamed of" (Marías 1988–1989, p. 284). My translation. The original Spanish text reads: "Debo decir que el libro me valió la amistad de varios jesuitas, que sintieron gratitud por el hecho de que hubiese señalado algo de que se avergonzaban".

[11] My translation. The original Spanish text reads: "El doctorado me sirvió, sobre todo, en países extranjeros, para no tener que explicar por qué no lo tenía".

of 1951. In 1953, Marías was elected member of the French *Institut International de Philosophie*, and in 1955, he was invited to teach a university course at the University of California at Los Angeles (UCLA). In 1956, he was invited professor at the University of Yale, where he was offered a permanent position as full professor, which he declined because he did not want to leave Spain. In his memoirs, Marías tells of this event, adding to it a touch of humour:

> Despite everything, the resolution grew in me to go back to Spain, to live in my country, inside my language, to carry on with all the things to which I had dedicated my life. I was sure that Lolita, even though she liked the United States, would not feel happy; and as for my sons, aged between two and eight years old, if I stayed they would certainly have become Americans. It will be said that this was an advantage; but they had been born Spaniards, and I did not feel authorised to change their destiny. Moreover, I thought that being a Spaniard, with some quality and dedication, is not a bad thing at all. And last, I really liked being a teacher of Americans, a friend of Americans; I would not have been displeased to be the grandfather of Americans; but the father of Americans was too much for me! At Yale University, they treated me with touching cordiality and esteem. They offered me a permanent post as *full professor*, under very attractive conditions. If I wanted to keep my hand in with Spanish studies, I could give a course in the Spanish department aside from the courses in the Philosophy department. If I accepted, everything would have been resolved, while back in Spain difficulties, risks, troubles and, worst of all, disappointments awaited me. But my decision to return was firm. (Marías 1988–1989, p. 372)[12]

---

[12] My translation. The original Spanish text reads: "A pesar de todo, se fue decantando en mí la resolución de volver a España, de vivir en mi país, dentro de mi lengua, de continuar todas las cosas a las que había puesto mi vida. Estaba seguro de que Lolita, aunque Estados Unidos le gustaban, no se sentiría feliz; en cuanto a mis hijos, entre ocho y dos años, si me quedaba serían sin duda americanos. Se dirá que esto era una ventaja; pero habían nacido españoles, y no me sentía autorizado a cambiar su destino. Además, pensaba que el ser español, con alguna calidad y esmero, no está nada mal. Finalmente, me gustaba mucho ser profesor de americanos, amigo de americanos; no me hubiera desagradado ser abuelo de americanos; pero ¡padre de americanos me parecía demasiado! La Universidad de Yale se portó conmigo con una cordialidad y estimación conmovedoras. Me ofreció un puesto permanente de *full professor*, en condiciones muy atractivas. Si no quería romper con los estudios españoles, podía dar, además de los cursos del departamento de Filosofía, uno en el de Español. Si aceptaba, lo tenía todo resuelto, mientras que en España me esperaban dificultades, riesgos, sinsabores y, lo peor de todo, decepciones. Pero mi decisión de volver era inquebrantable".

Despite declining the position, Marías maintained a close relationship with the United States, regularly giving courses and lectures at different universities across the country. Stemming from his frequent trips to the United States, Marías wrote two books commenting on different aspects of North American society: *Los Estados Unidos en escorzo* (Marías 1956b) [*The United States in Foreshortening*] and *Análisis de los Estados Unidos* (Marías 1968) [*Analysis of the United States*], which were later translated into English and published in the same volume under the name *America in the Fifties and Sixties: Julián Marías on the United States* (Marías 1972).

During the 1950s and 1960s, Marías also achieved greater recognition in Spain. To this effect, in 1965 he was elected member of the *Real Academia Española* ("Royal Spanish Academy")—and this while he was still excluded from the Spanish university system.

The decades of the 1950s and 1960s can be considered the period of intellectual maturation of Marías's philosophical thought. Among his philosophical works produced in these years, worth mentioning is his essay *Idea de la metafísica* (Marías 1954b) [*The Idea of Metaphysics* (Marías 1954a)] and the set of papers originally written in Spanish but later republished in their English translation in the compilation entitled *Philosophy as a Dramatic Theory* (Marías 1971). Most of these essays already include some of the central philosophical theses that Marías would develop in a systematic and coherent way in his book *Antropología metafísica: la estructura empírica de la vida humana* (Marías 1970d) [*Metaphysical Anthropology: The Empirical Structure of Human Life* (Marías 1970c)] (hereafter referred to as *Antropología metafísica*), which should be considered his most original and philosophically relevant work. In fact, most of the philosophical claims he would later develop until the end of his life are already schematically present in *Antropología metafísica*. Marías himself considers *Antropología metafísica* his major philosophical work:

> [...] [*Antropología metafísica*] was to be the most personal and original of all the [books] I had written up until then. I was convinced that this philosophical book was to be, *in the long run*, the most important thing I was doing, the best and most opportune thing I could do. I finished it on 23rd March 1970. Two months later it came out in Spanish; a year later in

English and in Portuguese, in the United States and Brazil. In several ways, to me it meant the beginning of a new phase. [...] *Antropología metafísica* was rather a watershed. It was possible at a precise moment in my life; it reworked my past and put it in a different light, opening up perspectives that until then were not possible. [...] It should not be too surprising that a life stage is marked not by a revolution, an economic crisis or a love passion, but by a level of thought. (Marías 1988–1989, pp. 538 *and* 547, author's emphasis)[13]

As will be covered in Chap. 3, Marías's Metaphysical Anthropology expands in an innovative and philosophically relevant way on Ortega's ontological claim that *my life* ("*mi vida*") is the *radical reality* ("*realidad radical*") in the sense of it being the primary and fundamental reality in which all other realities are *radicated* ("rooted"). Very briefly, Marías's Metaphysical Anthropology aims to study the realisation of *human life* in the form of *man*. Marías named his position as Metaphysical Anthropology because the apprehension of the determinations that are constitutive of the realisation of *human life* in the form of *man*—the concretisation of what Marías named as the *empirical structure of human life* ("*estructura empírica de la vida humana*"), and whose knowledge is obtained empirically—presupposes apprehension of the necessary conditions without which there is no *human life*—what Marías named as the *analytical structure of human life* ("*estructura analítica de la vida humana*"), and whose knowledge is obtained through metaphysical analysis of *my life*.

After Franco's death at the age of 82 on 20th November 1975, the regime change that saw Spain progress from the Francoist dictatorship to the consolidation of a democratic parliamentary system in the form of a constitutional monarchy began. This period in Spain's recent history

---

[13] My translation. The Spanish original text reads: "[...] iba a ser el más personal y original de cuantos había escrito hasta entonces. Estaba persuadido de que este libro filosófico era *a la larga* lo más importante que estaba haciendo, lo mejor y más oportuno que podía hacer. Lo terminé el 23 de marzo de 1970. Dos meses después apareció en español; un año más tarde en inglés y en portugués, en Estados Unidos y en Brasil. En varios sentidos significaba para mí el comienzo de una nueva fase. [...] La *Antropología metafísica* significó algo así como una divisoria de aguas. Fue posible en un momento preciso de mi vida; reobró sobre su pasado y lo puso a otra luz, abrió perspectivas que hasta entonces no eran posibles. [...] No debe sorprender demasiado que una etapa vital esté marcada no por una revolución, una crisis económica o una pasión amorosa, sino por un nivel de pensamiento".

from 1975 to 1979 is commonly referred to in Spain as "*la transición*" ("the Transition"), given that the change of regime was not abrupt but was progressive and internal, with the regime's own juridical tools used to dismantle it. There were social and political tensions and even violent actions by some terrorist organisations, but it can be said that the process was generally peaceful—especially considering that the Francoist regime was the outcome of a civil war.

Two central events that took place during *la transición* must be highlighted. The first occurred in December 1976, when the so-called "*Ley para la Reforma Política*" ("Law for the Political Reform") was approved by referendum. The law allowed the elimination of the juridical basis of the Francoist regime from a legal point of view—that is, within the very same regime and so, formally speaking, without breaking the already established legality. The second event took place between 1977 and 1979. Following the approval of the *Ley para la Reforma Política*, there were general elections on 15th June 1977, in which all the members of the lower house and most of the members of the upper house were elected by universal suffrage. These elections were the first democratic general elections after more than 40 years of dictatorship, ushering in the so-called "*legislatura constituyente*" ("constituent legislature"), the exclusive aim of which was to eliminate the juridical basis of the Francoist regime and to draft (and approve) the first plenary Spanish democratic constitution following the dictatorship. On 21st July 1978, the Spanish Constitution was approved by the Spanish parliament. On 6th December 1978, it was ratified by referendum, formally entering into force on 29th December 1978. Shortly afterwards, general elections were called for March 1979, thereby marking democratic normality. Since then, Spain has been a fully-fledged democracy in the form of a constitutional monarchy.

During the *legislatura constituyente*, and still today, Spain had two legislative chambers, the Senate—the Upper House—and the Parliament—the Lower House, the official name of which is now "*Congreso de los Diputados*" ("Congress of Deputies"). Regarding the *legislatura constituyente*, all the members of the lower house were elected by universal suffrage, and while most of the members of the upper house were too, a fifth of them (a total of 41) were elected by direct royal appointment—an undemocratic aspect of the political system that was eliminated by the Constitution of 1978.

The Spanish King, Juan Carlos I (born 1938; reign 1975–2014), elected as senators personalities with intellectual relevance and prestige, regardless of their political persuasion. Among them was Marías, who by the 1970s was now recognised as one of the most notable philosophers of his generation. As a senator, Marías took part in discussions on and the approval of the Spanish Constitution of 1978. He also wrote several newspaper articles, some of which ended up influencing the final text of the Constitution. For example, in some of them Marías criticised the fact that in the first draft of the Constitution there was no explicit mention of Spain as a nation—which was most likely due to pressure from some of the Spanish regionalist political parties who wanted to reserve the use of the term for their respective regions. In his memoirs, Marías explains his position on this point as follows:

> I was especially concerned about something that seemed simply intolerable to me: the disappearance of the term "nation" applied to Spain, which was not used even once in the draft. I remembered that the first nation in the modern sense of the word had been Spain, that this term had been applied to it for centuries, and of course throughout all our constitutional history. [...] On the other hand, it seemed to me to be an error, both linguistically and politically, to speak of "nationalities" as the name of *some* Spanish regions, because *nationality* does not mean a society or a territory, but a property, affection or condition. With that improper word it was intended to set aside the word "nation", as has been seen since then ad nauseam. (Marías 1988–1989, pp. 660–661, author's emphasis; see also: Marías 1998, pp. 428–435 *and* 521–525)[14]

---

[14] My translation. The Spanish original text reads: "Me inquietó sobre todo algo que me parecía simplemente intolerable: la desaparición del nombre 'nación' aplicado a España, que no se usaba ni una sola vez en el anteproyecto. Recordé que la primera nación en el sentido moderno de la palabra había sido España, que este nombre se le había aplicado durante siglos, y por supuesto en toda nuestra historia constitucional. [...] En cambio, me parecía un error, tanto lingüístico como político, hablar de 'nacionalidades' como nombre de *algunas* regiones españolas, ya que *nacionalidad* no significa una sociedad o territorio, sino una propiedad, afección o condición. Con esa palabra impropia se trataba de deslizar la de 'nación', como se ha visto después hasta la saciedad".

Partially triggered by these articles, lively political debate ensued on the issue, concluding with explicit mention in the final draft of the Constitution of "the indissoluble unity of the Spanish Nation, the common and indivisible homeland of all Spaniards", while also recognising and guaranteeing "the right to autonomy of the nationalities and regions of which it is composed and the solidarity among them all" (Art. 2).[15] Many of the articles that Marías wrote during these years where later compiled in his book *La España real* (Marías 1998)—originally published in four separate volumes between years 1976 and 1981, and whose title, in reference to the current form of Spain as a constitutional monarchy, plays on the two meanings of the Spanish word "*real*", "real" and "royal", meaning that the title of *La España real* can be translated in English as either *The Real Spain* or *The Royal Spain*. Last, it is worth mentioning that during his time as member of the upper house, Marías achieved considerable popularity among the general, non-philosophical public, taking part in cultural TV programmes in addition to writing newspaper articles.

Once the *legislatura constituyente* ended, Marías left his position as member of the upper house. Shortly afterwards, he was offered a position as Professor of Philosophy at the then recently created Universidad Nacional de Educación a Distancia, UNED. Marías accepted the position, teaching there from 1980 until his retirement in 1984 at the age of 70. Nonetheless, and almost until the date of his death in 2005 at the age of 91, Marías remained intellectually active, giving courses and conferences both in Spain and abroad, and above all continuing to write philosophical books which, in one way or another, expanded on the original claims made in *Antropología metafísica*. Among his late works, and given the purposes of this book, we must highlight two: *La felicidad humana* (Marías 1987a) [*The Human Happiness*], in which he extensively develops his own conception of human happiness and its connection with death

---

[15] The quotes are from the official English translation made by the Spanish upper house, the original Spanish text reading: "la indisolube unidad de la Nación española, patria común e indivisible de todos los españoles" and "el derecho a la autonomía de las nacionalidades y regiones que la integran y la solidaridad entre todas ellas". As of October 2023, both the original Spanish text and the English translation can be consulted in the official website of the Spanish upper house: https://www.senado.es/web/conocersenado/normas/constitucion/index.html?lang=es_ES (Spanish original text); https://www.senado.es/web/conocersenado/normas/constitucion/index.html?lang=en (English official translation).

and the call for personal immortality he had already argued in *Antropología metafísica*; and *La perspectiva cristiana* (Marías 1999b) [*The Christian Perspective* (Marías 1999a)], in which he offers his own analysis of the contents of Christian Revelation.

References

Basallo, A. (n.d.). Bibliografía cinematográfica de Julián Marías. *Biblioteca Virtual Miguel de Cervantes*. https://www.cervantesvirtual.com/portales/julian_marias/su_obra_cinematografica. Accessed December 2023.

Instituto de Humanidades (1948) 1961. Prospecto del Instituto de Humanidades. In *José Ortega y Gasset: Obras Completas (vol. VII: 1948–1958)*, 9–24. Madrid: Revista de Occidente.

Marías, J. (1941a) 2020. *Gatry's Philosophy*. Trans. Mary L O'Hare. Hindmarsh: ATF Press Publishing.

Marías, J. (1941b) 1959. La filosofía del Padre Gatry. In *Julián Marías: Obras (vol. IV)*, 146–314. Madrid: Revista de Occidente.

Marías, J. (1941c) 1967. *History of Philosophy*. Trans. Stanley Appelbaum and Clarence Strombridge. New York: Dover Publications.

Marías, J. (1941d) 1958. Historia de la Filosofía. In *Julián Marías: Obras (vol. I)*, 1–475. Madrid: Revista de Occidente.

Marías, J. (1943a) 1966. *Miguel de Unamuno*. Trans. Frances M. López-Morillas. Cambridge, Massachusetts: Harvard University Press.

Marías, J. (1943b) 1960. Miguel de Unamuno. In *Julián Marías: Obras (vol. V)*, 1–201. Madrid: Revista de Occidente.

Marías, J. (1947a) 1956. *Reason and Life: The Introduction to Philosophy*. Trans. Kenneth S. Reid and Edward Sarmiento. London: Hollis and Carter.

Marías, J. (1947b) 1962. Introducción a la Filosofía. In *Julián Marías: Obras (vol. II)*, xv–367. Madrid: Revista de Occidente.

Marías, J. (1948). *Filosofía española actual (Unamuno, Ortega, Morente, Zubiri)*. Buenos Aires: Espasa-Calpe.

Marías, J. (1950a) 1954. Presence and Absence of Existentialism in Spain. *Philosophy and Phenomenological Research* 15 (2): 180–191. Trans. Janet Aronson Weiss.

Marías, J. (1950b) 1960. Presencia y ausencia del existencialismo en España. In *Julián Marías: Obras (vol. V)*, 217–231. Madrid: Revista de Occidente.

Marías, J. (1950c). *Ortega y tres antípodas: un ejemplo de intriga intellectual.* Buenos Aires: Revista de Occidente Argentina.

Marías, J. (1952) 1959. El problema de la libertad intelectual. In *Julián Marías: Obras (vol. IV)*, 485–500. Madrid: Revista de Occidente.

Marías, J. (1954a) 1967. The Idea of Metaphysics. In *Contemporary Spanish Philosophy: An Anthology*, trans. and ed. A. Robert Caponigri, 324–370. Notre Dame: University of Notre Dame Press.

Marías, J. (1954b) 1962. Idea de la metafísica. In *Julián Marías: Obras (vol. II)*, 369–413. Madrid: Revista de Occidente.

Marías, J. (1956a) 1960. La imagen de la vida humana. In *Julián Marías: Obras (vol. V)*, 509–571. Madrid: Revista de Occidente.

Marías, J. (1956b) 1964. Los Estados Unidos en escorzo. In *Julián Marías: Obras (vol. III)*, 349–545. Madrid: Revista de Occidente.

Marías, J. (1959) 1960. La escuela de Madrid. In *Julián Marías: Obras (vol. V)*, 203–507. Madrid: Revista de Occidente.

Marías, J. (1968) 1970. Análisis de los Estados Unidos. In *Julián Marías: Obras (vol. VIII)*, 11–137. Madrid: Revista de Occidente.

Marías, J. (1970a). *Visto y no visto (vol. I: 1962–1964).* Madrid: Ediciones Guadarrama.

Marías, J. (1970b). *Visto y no visto (vol. II: 1965–1967).* Madrid: Ediciones Guadarrama.

Marías, J. (1970c) 1971. *Metaphysical Anthropology: The Empirical Structure of Human Life.* Trans. Frances M. López-Morillas. Pennsylvania: The Pennsylvania State University Press.

Marías, J. (1970d). *Antropología metafísica: la estructura empírica de la vida humana.* Madrid: Revista de Occidente.

Marías, J. (1971). *Philosophy as Dramatic Theory.* Trans. James Parsons. Pennsylvania: The Pennsylvania State University Press.

Marías, J. (1972). *America in the Fifties and Sixties: Julián Marías on the United States.* Trans. Blanche de Puy and Harold C. Raley. Pennsylvania: The Pennsylvania State University Press.

Marías, J. (1987a). *La felicidad humana.* Madrid: Alianza Editorial.

Marías, J. (1987b) 1989. *A felicidade humana.* Trans. Diva Ribeiro de Toledo Piza. São Paulo: Livraria Duas Cidades.

Marías, J. (1987c) 1990. *La felicità umana.* Trans. Grazia e Luigi Ferrero de G. V. Torino: Edizioni Paoline.

Marías, J. (1988–1989) 2017. *Una vida presente: Memorias.* Madrid: Páginas de Espuma.

Marías, J. (1994). *El cine de Julián Marías. Volumen I. Escritos sobre cine (1960–1965)*, ed. Fernando Alonso. Barcelona: Royal Books.

Marías, J. (1998). *La España Real*. Madrid: Editorial Espasa Calpe.

Marías, J. (1999a) 2000. *The Christian Perspective*. Trans. Harold Raley. Houston: Halcyon Press.

Marías, J. (1999b). *La perspectiva cristiana*. Madrid: Alianza Editorial.

Marías, J. (2000). *Tratado sobre la convivencia. Concordia sin acuerdo*. Barcelona: Ediciones Martínez Roca.

Oya, A. (2022). Joaquim Xirau: amor, persona y mundo. *Bulletin of Hispanic Studies* 99 (9): 835–843.

Roldán Sarmiento, P. (2007). Bibliografía de Julián Marías (libros y ensayos). In *Julián Marías. Una filosofía en libertad*, ed. José María Atencia Páez, 303–315. Málaga: Servicio de Publicaciones e Intercambio Científico de la Universidad de Málaga (SPICUM).

3

The Metaphysical Anthropology of Julián Marías

Abstract This chapter offers a detailed account of Julián Marías's Metaphysical Anthropology. It begins with a short introduction pointing out that his Metaphysical Anthropology expands on José Ortega y Gasset's ontological claim that *"my life"* (*"mi vida"*) is the *"radical reality"* (*"realidad radical"*). The chapter is divided into two sections. In the first section ("José Ortega y Gasset: *My Life* as the *Radical Reality*), Ortega's argument for claiming that *my life* (each one's) is the fundamental and primary reality is analysed; the second section ("Julián Marías: The Empirical Structure of Human Life") contains a detailed account of Marías's Metaphysical Anthropology.

Keywords Analytical structure • Empirical structure • Human life • Installation • José Ortega y Gasset • Julián Marías • Man • Metaphysical Anthropology (*"Antropología metafísica"*) • My life (*"Mi vida"*) • Radical reality (*"Realidad radical"*)

This chapter offers a detailed account of Julián Marías's Metaphysical Anthropology, which expands in an innovative and philosophically

© The Author(s), under exclusive license to Springer Nature Switzerland AG 2024
A. Oya, *The Metaphysical Anthropology of Julián Marías*, Palgrave Frontiers in Philosophy of Religion, https://doi.org/10.1007/978-3-031-61804-8_3

relevant way on José Ortega y Gasset's ontological claim that *"my life"* (*"mi vida"*) is the *"radical reality"* (*"realidad radical"*). In brief, and the precise meaning of which will become clear later, the subject matter of Marías's Metaphysical Anthropology is the study of the realisation of *human life* in the form of *man*.

Marías's Metaphysical Anthropology is systematically formulated in his book *Antropología metafísica: la estructura empírica de la vida humana* (Marías 1970b) [*Metaphysical Anthropology: The Empirical Structure of Human Life* (Marías 1970a)] (hereafter referred to as *Antropología metafísica*). The book was first published in 1970, but its origins can be traced back to Marías's writings from the 1950s and 1960s—especially to his book *Idea de la metafísica* (Marías 1954b) [*The Idea of Metaphysics* (Marías 1954a)] and to the set of essays that were later translated into English and included in the compilation *Philosophy as a Dramatic Theory* (Marías 1971).

Antropología metafísica should be seen as Marías's major philosophical work, Marías himself, as already mentioned in Chap. 2, considering it as such. In fact, most of the philosophical books Marías published after *Antropología metafísica* in some way or another all aim to substantially develop the core claims that were already present in this book, albeit in a much more schematised formulation.

As already mentioned, Marías's Metaphysical Anthropology expands on Ortega's claim that *my life* is the *radical reality*, which is why the first section of this chapter is dedicated to analysing Ortega's argument for reaching this conclusion. However, it should be emphasised that Marías's Metaphysical Anthropology, while having Ortega as its starting point, is a complete original philosophical position of his. Marías was, of course, well aware that he was expanding Ortega's philosophy in an innovative way not present in Ortega's works:

> For the moment I shall give the expression "human life" the meaning which it really has in language when we use it spontaneously, without reservation and without scientific intent. This is precisely what Ortega did, and in this sense the reference to his thought is permissible. When I use this name I am designating *the same thing*—that is, the same reality— which he named with that word. But this does not imply that the content

of what I am going to say is "the same philosophy". Rather, it excludes my doing so. [...] In fact, I am going to take up as a principal theme the analysis and recognition of one stratum of the reality which is human life that has not been studied in Ortega's work; something to which I first called attention more than twenty years ago, and which has not yet been adequately explored. In this sense, these investigations—like all of my work in general—are intended to be added to Ortega: not to forget him, nor to be subtracted from him, nor to start from zero—for to do so it would be necessary, of course, to have previously annulled him, and this would be neither easy nor interesting nor fruitful. (Marías 1970a, p. 46, author's emphasis [Marías 1970b, pp. 58–59])

3.1 José Ortega y Gasset: *My Life* as the *Radical Reality*

The aim of this section is to analyse the main philosophical thesis Ortega defended, which is that of conceiving *my life* ("*mi vida*") as the *radical reality* ("*realidad radical*")—in the sense of it being the fundamental and primary reality in which any other realities are *radicated* ("rooted").

Before entering into the aforementioned philosophical issue, allow me to briefly introduce José Ortega y Gasset, and especially some of his most well-known works. José Ortega y Gasset was born in Madrid in 1883. In 1910, having finished his studies in Philosophy at the Universities of Madrid (1899–1904), Leipzig and Berlin (1905–1906), and Marburgo (1906–1907 and 1911), he took up the Chair of Metaphysics at Universidad Central de Madrid. In 1914, Ortega published his first book, entitled *Meditaciones del Quijote* (Ortega y Gasset 1914b) [*Meditations on Quixote* (Ortega y Gasset 1914a)]. Although in it Ortega's philosophy is not yet explicitly and systematically formulated, this book already contains the formula used to schematically summarise Ortega's philosophy: "*Yo soy yo y mi circunstancia, y si no la salvo a ella no me salvo yo*" ("I am myself and my circumstance, and if I do not save it I do not save myself") (Ortega y Gasset 1914b, p. 322 [Ortega y Gasset 1914a, p. 45]). Ortega soon gained popularity for his newspaper articles commenting on the tumultuous political situation in the Spain of the time.

In 1922, as a set of articles in the Spanish newspaper *El Sol* and later compiled in a book, Ortega published his essay *España invertebrada* (Ortega y Gasset 1922b) [*Invertebrate Spain* (Ortega y Gasset 1922a)], which had a considerable impact on the political and intellectual climate of the time. In it, Ortega argued that one of Spain's fundamental problems was its persistent "hatred towards the best" ("*odio a los mejores*"), its "aristophobia" ("*aristofobia*"). The analysis offered in *España invertebrada* is connected with the core claim of what is now probably his most well-known essay both nationally and internationally, *La rebelión de las masas* (Ortega y Gasset 1929b) [*The Revolt of the Masses* (Ortega y Gasset 1929a)]. Published in 1929, in it Ortega claimed that the most characteristic and peculiar trait of twentieth century society was that it suffered from the total domination of the masses of mediocre men—the "*hombre masa*" ("mass-man"), as Ortega collectively named them. Previously, in 1923, Ortega had published the essay *El tema de nuestro tiempo* (Ortega y Gasset 1923b) [*The Modern Theme* (Ortega y Gasset 1923a)], which aimed to put an end to the philosophical controversy between realism and idealism. In 1957, the book *¿Qué es Filosofía?* (Ortega y Gasset 1957b) [*What Is Philosophy?* (Ortega y Gasset 1957a)] was posthumously published, containing eleven lectures that Ortega gave in Madrid in 1929, most of them previously unpublished. In these conferences, Ortega summarised in a coherent and systematic way his own philosophical views—which, in general lines, did not thereafter undergo any major changes. José Ortega y Gasset died in Madrid in 1955, although from the start of the Francoist Regime his official residence had been in Portugal. Another point worth mentioning is that Ortega y Gasset is commonly considered as the most outstanding intellectual figure of the Spanish "*generación del 27*" ("Generation of the 27th"). As mentioned in Chap. 2, his works have had a deep influence on thinkers like Manuel García Morente (1886–1942), Xavier Zubiri (1898–1983) and Julián Marías (1914–2005), who configured the so-called *Escuela de Madrid* ("School of Madrid"). Ortega, together with Miguel de Unamuno (1864–1936), is one of the twentieth century's two generally accepted best-known Spanish philosophers. His audience is not restricted to Spanish speaking countries, but his works have managed to reach an international educated readership—several of his articles and most of his books having been translated into English and other major languages.

After this short biographical note, we will now turn to Ortega's philosophy. To the classic controversy between naive realism, which claims that the world is a reality subsistent in itself and so completely independent of the concrete subject, and idealism, which claims that the conscience, the thinking I, is the most primary reality, Ortega responded by arguing that the primary and fundamental reality is neither the world nor the I, but the coexistence between the world and the I—a position which is schematically summarised in Ortega's formula "*Yo soy yo y mi circunstancia, y si no la salvo a ella no me salvo* yo" ("I am myself and my circumstance, and if I do not save it I do not save myself") (Ortega y Gasset 1914b, p. 322 [Ortega y Gasset 1914a, p. 45]).

The world, as it appears to me, is not independent of me. The reason why the world appears to me as being such and such and not otherwise is precisely, Ortega claims, because I am representing the world in some given way and not another. The world, then, "exhausts its being in its appearance" (Ortega y Gasset 1957a, p. 198 [Ortega y Gasset 1957b, p. 402]). According to Ortega, this is the valid intuition behind idealism—that is, that "the world is not a reality subsisting in itself and independent of me—it is what it is *for* me, and for the moment is nothing more" (Ortega y Gasset 1957a, p. 198, author's emphasis [Ortega y Gasset 1957b, p. 402]). I represent the world—and the world thereby lacks an independent reality on its own because the way the world appears to me to be is dependent on my representing it. However, the world is not *my* representing it, but what is represented—that is, the world is not reduced to my representational activity, the thinking I.[1] In fact, Ortega argues that neither is my representing the world, the thinking I, a substantial reality on its own, since there cannot be representing without something being represented, and despite *my* representing emerging from myself, the thinking I, what is represented is not reduced to me. In short, I cannot represent without my representing being a representation *of something*, and that something is not me. The fundamental reality is not, then, either the world, as naive realism claims, or the thinking I, as

---

[1] See Ortega's claim that "I represent the world to myself. What is mine is the act of representing, and this is what representation clearly means. But the world which I represent to myself is not my representing, but the thing which is represented. My part is the representing, not the represented" (Ortega y Gasset 1957a, pp. 196–197 [Ortega y Gasset 1957b, p. 401]).

idealism claims, but rather the coexistence between the world and the I. Ortega summarises his argument as follows:

> The basic datum of the Universe is not simply that either thought exists or I, the thinker, exist, but that if thought exists, *ipso facto*, I who think and the world about which I think also exist; the one exists with the other, having no possible separation between them. I am not a substantial being nor is the world, but we both are in active correlation; I am that which sees the world and the world is that which is seen by me. I exist for the world, and the world exists for me. If there were no things to be seen, thought about, and imagined, I would not see, think, or imagine; that is to say, I would not exist. (Ortega y Gasset 1957a, p. 199 [Ortega y Gasset 1957b, pp. 402–403])[2]

This is the reason why Ortega claims that the coexistence between the world and the I, what he refers to as "*mi vida*" ("my life"), is the fundamental reality, "the most radical way of being" ("*el modo de ser más radical*") (Ortega y Gasset 1957b, p. 405).[3] Here it should be noted that Ortega uses the term "*radical*" in its meaning of "belonging or relating to the root". Everything I can relate to, be it theoretically or practically, is "rooted in" ("*radicado en*"), and so determined by, the coexistence between myself and the world—as Ortega puts it, "Every other thing, every other manner of being I find within my own life, both as a detail of it and with reference to it. In it is all the rest, and all the rest is what it is with regard to that life" (Ortega y Gasset 1957a, p. 202 [Ortega y Gasset 1957b, p. 405]).

As mentioned before, Ortega's claim that *my life* (each one's) is the *radical reality* is schematically summarised in the formula "*Yo soy yo y mi circunstancia, y si no la salvo a ella no me salvo yo*", which has been translated into English in two different ways. When only the first part of the formula is quoted ("*Yo soy yo y mi circunstancia*"), it is commonly

---

[2] See also: "[The world] is not inside my thought and forming part of it, but neither is it outside my thought if by outside one understands having nothing to do with it—it is inseparably linked with my thinking of it, neither outside my thought nor within it, but linked with it; as is inverse with reverse, left with right; yet right is not left nor is reverse the same as inverse" (Ortega y Gasset 1957a, p. 197 [Ortega y Gasset 1957b, p. 401]).

[3] Adam's translation is inaccurate here. He translates "el modo de ser más radical" as "To live is the process of going down to the roots" (Ortega y Gasset 1957a, p. 202). A more accurate translation is "the most radical way of being".

translated into English as "I am I and my circumstance". However, when the whole formula is quoted ("*Yo soy yo y mi circunstancia, y si no la salvo a ella no me salvo yo*"), the most usual English translation is "I am myself and my circumstance, and if I do not save it I do not save myself". Interestingly, this second English translation discloses the distinction between the first "*yo*" and the second and third times "*yo*" appears in Ortega's formula, which is not made explicit in its original Spanish expression. The first "*yo*" refers to *my life* as *radical reality*, whereas the second and third uses refer to I myself, the executive I who deals with the circumstance.

Ortega's claim that the most primary reality is "'my life', 'our life', the life of every one of us" (Ortega y Gasset 1957a, p. 202 [Ortega y Gasset 1957b, p. 405]), does not, according to him, preclude the possibility of other realities. These other realities should be considered as, so to say, second-degree realities inasmuch as they are *radicated* ("rooted") in the most basic and primary reality that is *my life*. However, this does not diminish their reality. Ortega makes this point when he claims that

> [...] one property of the radical reality that is my life is that it contains within it many presumed realities, or realities of the second order—a fact that opens to my life an immense field of realities different from it. For by calling them, loosely, presumed—we could also say "probable"—I do not deprive them of the character and value of realities. I deny them only the quality of being *radical* or unquestionable realities. So it appears that the attribution of reality allows and even demands a scale or gradation or hierarchy and that there will be, as with burns, first-degree realities, second-degree realities, and so on—the reference, however, being not to the content of the given reality but to its pure character of being reality. (Ortega y Gasset 1957c, p. 95, author's emphasis [Ortega y Gasset 1957d, p. 142])[4]

---

[4] See also: "Calling it 'radical reality' does not mean that it is the only reality, nor even the highest, worthiest or most sublime, nor yet the supreme reality, but simply that it is the root of all other realities, in the sense that they—any of them—in order to be reality to us must in some way make themselves present, or at least announce themselves, within the shaken confines of our own life. Hence this radical reality—my life—is so little 'egoistic', so far from 'solipsistic', that in essence it is the open area, the waiting stage, on which any other reality may manifest itself and celebrate its Pentecost. God himself, to be God to us, must somehow or other proclaim his existence to us, and that is why he thunders on Sinai, lashes the money-changers in the temple court, and sails on the three-masted frigate of Golgotha" (Ortega y Gasset 1957c, p. 40 [Ortega y Gasset 1957d, 101]).

Besides, *my life* (and each one's life) is neither an abstraction nor a concrete fact but a "task" (*"un quehacer"*), consisting in my engaging with and relating to the world I coexist with—that is, "in occupying myself with this my world, in seeing it, imagining it, thinking about it, loving it, hating it, being sad or being happy in it and through it, in moving about in it, in transforming it and in suffering from it" (Ortega y Gasset 1957a, p. 201 [Ortega y Gasset 1957b, p. 404]). This is what Ortega meant when claiming that "Man is no thing, but a drama":

> Man is not his body, which is a thing, nor his soul, psyche, conscience, or spirit, which is also a thing. Man is no thing, but a drama—his life, a pure and universal happening which happens to each one of us and in which each one in his turn is nothing but happening. [...] Life is a gerundive, not a participle: a *faciendum*, not a *factum*. Life is a task. (Ortega y Gasset 1935a, pp. 199–200 [Ortega y Gasset 1935b, pp. 32–33])[5]

According to Ortega, then, *my life* is not a thing, a *res*, but a task, an activity (*"un quehacer"*). It consists in my dealing with my circumstance, the world I happen to coexist with. However, my dealing with my circumstance is not an automatic mechanical process, but requires an active and conscious decision by my part. I (and each one of us) should decide each time how to deal with my (each one's) circumstance. At each moment I must decide how I am going to act next—explaining Ortega's claim that *my life* is *"preocupación"* ("preoccupation") and so *"futurismo"* ("futurism"):

> Whether we like it or not, our life is in its very essence futurism. [...] I say that life is preoccupation, and not only in moments which are difficult, but all the time; in essence it is no more than this, to be preoccupied. Every moment of the day we are having to decide what we are going to do the next moment, what it is that will occupy our lives. This is occupying our-

---

[5] See also: "Man *is* not, he 'goes on being' this and that. The concept 'to go on being' is, however, absurd: under promise of something logical it turns out in the end to be completely irrational. The term we can apply, without absurdity, to 'going on being' is 'living'. Let us say, then, not that man *is*, but that he *lives*" (Ortega y Gasset 1935a, p. 213, author's emphasis [Ortega y Gasset 1935b, p. 39]).

selves in anticipation, pre-occupying ourselves. (Ortega y Gasset 1957a, pp. 247 *and* 249 [Ortega y Gasset 1957b, pp. 435 *and* 436])

Given that living is not a mechanical, automatic process, an active and conscious decision on the part of the concrete individual is always necessary. Each of us can decide to act in the way we feel is the most appropriate. In this regard, according to Ortega, we are actually free to choose our own path of action (hence of being). The only thing we are not free to do is to avoid the task of deciding how to act—meaning that we are not just free but *forced* to be free. This is what Ortega meant when claiming that "[…] man is the only reality that does not simply consist in being but must choose its own being" (Ortega y Gasset 1957c, p. 44 [Ortega y Gasset 1957d, p. 103]):

> […] circumstance always offers us different possibilities for acting, hence for being. This obliges us, like it or not, to exercise our freedom. We are forced to be free. Because of this, life is a permanent crossroads and constant perplexity. At every instant we have to choose whether in the next instant or at some other future time we shall be he who does this or he who does that. Hence each of us is incessantly choosing his "doing", hence his being. (Ortega y Gasset 1957c, p. 58 [Ortega y Gasset 1957d, p. 114])

In order to act, then, a previous contemplative or reflective individual exercise is required so as to carry out the *decision* about how I am going to deal with the circumstance I happen to coexist with. Ortega refers to this reflective process using the Spanish word "*ensimismamiento*", which he acknowledges to be a word exclusive to the Spanish language, although he vaguely identifies it with "the *vita contemplativa* of the Romans" and "the *theoretikos bios* of the Greeks" (Ortega y Gasset 1957c, p. 23 [Ortega y Gasset 1957d, p. 88]). Willard R. Trask, the English translator of *El hombre y la gente* (Ortega y Gasset 1957d) [*Man and People* (Ortega y Gasset 1957c)], translates "*ensimismamiento*" as "being in one's self", while pointing out that the literal English translation is "within-oneself-ness". Whatever the English word used, what is important to emphasise is that "*ensimismamiento*" does not refer to a meditative introspective state in which one passively becomes absorbed in, but rather to a reflective or meditative exercise that one consciously and actively decides to carry out. "*Ensimismamiento*", Ortega argues, is the necessary precondition for action. At every moment we find ourselves dominated by the circumstance with no clue as to how to deal with it, like a shipwrecked man in the sea with no foothold. There is no predetermined way to act but we should, by ourselves alone, *decide* what to do. To take such a decision, Ortega argues, "*ensimismamiento*" is required; that is, man should "[…] virtually and provisionally withdrawing himself from the world and taking his stand inside himself […]" (Ortega y Gasset 1957c, p. 18 [Ortega y Gasset 1957d, p. 84]). This allows us to *imagine* the different possibilities of acting (hence of being) available to us and decide which feels to us the most appropriate to follow. After this inward reflective exercise, we so to speak "come back" to the world with a preconceived plan of acting, of dealing with our (each one's) own circumstance. In Ortega's words:

> There are, then, three different moments, which are repeated cyclically throughout the course of human history, in forms each time more complex and rich: 1. Man feels himself lost, shipwrecked among things; this is *alteración*. 2. Man, by an energic effort, withdraws into himself to form ideas about things and possible ways of dominating them; this is being within one's self, *ensimismamiento*, the *vita contemplativa* of the Romans, the *theoretikos bios* of the Greeks, *theory*. 3. Man again submerges himself in the world, to act in it according to a preconceived plan; this is action, *vita activa, praxis*. Accordingly, *it is impossible to speak of action except in so far as it will be governed by a previous contemplation; and vice versa, contemplation, or being within one's self, is nothing but a projecting of future action.* (Ortega y Gasset 1957c, p. 23, author's emphasis [Ortega y Gasset 1957d, p. 88])[6]

This intimate and reflective exercise in which the "*ensimismamiento*" consists of allows us to enjoy of a self-governed life. Thanks to the capacity of "*ensimismamiento*" we are now not simply swept away by the whims of our circumstance, as are those who are shipwrecked in the middle of

---

[6] Willard R. Trask explains his decision for preserving the Spanish term *alteración* in his translation as follows: "Literally, 'otheration'. The Spanish word has, in addition to the meaning of English 'alteration', that of 'state of tumult', 'being beside oneself'" (Ortega y Gasset 1957c, p. 17).

the sea with no foothold, but we (at least try to) dominate the circumstance—which amounts to an (attempt) at self-affirmation, a positive endorsement of one's own singularity no matter what the circumstance is. The capacity of "*ensimismamiento*" is, according to Ortega, what marks the difference between man and the animal. Animals lack of a preconceived plan of action and so their behaviour is nothing more than an irreflective, mechanised reaction to the circumstance they happen to coexist with—they do not project themselves onto the world but rather they simply "stay there", and so their whole life is enslaved by the whims of the circumstance:

> The animal, in short, lives in perpetual fear of the world, and at the same time in a perpetual hunger for the things that are in the world and appear in the world, an ungovernable hunger that also discharges itself without any possible restraint or inhibition, just as the animal's fear does. In either case it is the objects and events in its environment which govern the animal's life, which pull and push it about like a marionette. It does not rule its life, it does not live from *itself*, but is always intent on what is happening outside it, on all that is *other* than itself. The word for "other" in Spanish— *otro*—is nothing but the Latin *alter*. To say, then, that the animal lives not from *itself* but from what is *other* than itself, pulled and pushed and tyrannized over by that *other*, is equivalent to saying that the animal is always estranged from itself, beside itself, that its life is essential *alteración*—possession by all that is *other*. […] The animal is pure *alteración*. It cannot be within itself. Hence when things cease to threaten it or caress it; when they give it a holiday; in short, when what is *other* ceases to move it and manage it, the poor animal has virtually to stop existing, that is, it goes to sleep. Hence the enormous capacity for somnolence that the animal exhibits, the infrahuman torpor which primitive man continues in part; and, on the other hand, the increasing insomnia of civilized man, the almost permanent, sometimes terrible and uncontrollable wakefulness which afflicts men of an intense inner life. (Ortega y Gasset 1957c, pp. 16–17 *and* 19, author's emphasis [Ortega y Gasset 1957d, pp. 83 *and* 85])

Our decision to act in such a way and not in another in its turn reflects what Ortega names as our own "program of life"—that is, the kind of man or woman each one of us has decided we want to be. The sort of "program of life" one decides to execute may not be an original invention on our part since it may be influenced by the social context one happens to be immersed in, but it still requires an active and more or less conscious decision on the part of the concrete individual. Each of us should decide what conception of life feels the most appropriate. This is what Ortega meant when claiming that "Whether he be original or plagiarist, man is the novelist of himself" (Ortega y Gasset 1935a, p. 203 [Ortega y Gasset 1935b, p. 34]). Moreover, the ability to act accordingly to the chosen "program of life" is in its turn the mark of an authentic life:

> Escape is possible from every circumstance, even the most extreme. What there is no escaping is having to do something and above all having to do what in the last analysis is the most difficult and painful of things—choosing, preferring. How many times have we not told ourselves that we should prefer not to prefer? From which it follows that what is given me when life is given me is simply "things to do". Life, as we all know only too well, "takes a lot of doing". And the most important thing is to make sure that what we choose to do in each case is not *just anything*, but the thing that has to be done—done here and now—that it is our true vocation, our genuine "thing to do". (Ortega y Gasset 1957c, pp. 45–46, author's emphasis [Ortega y Gasset 1957d, p. 104]; see also: Ortega y Gasset 1957c, p. 29 [Ortega y Gasset 1957d, p. 92])

However, it should be noted that (each one's) "program of life" is not invariable, but changes with the passage of time. Sometimes a "program of life" is simply abandoned for a completely different one. Throughout life, in our dealing with our (each one of us's) circumstance, we put into practice different "programs of life", and the experiences we get from this trial-and-error end up modifying our ideal of the type of man or woman we want to become. This is what, as Ortega rightly points out, in everyday language is called "experience of life" (Ortega y Gasset 1935a, p. 209 [Ortega y Gasset 1935b, p. 37]). The kind of man I wanted to become ten years ago is not the exact same kind of man I *now* want to become—and even assuming that I will not suffer any tragic event, it seems irremediable that some of my current vital goals will have changed in some way or another ten years from now. Our past experiences affect our present and future actions in a negative way, determining the kind of man we *no longer* want to be. We have put into practice projects of being that, for some reason, we have decided to abandon. Abandoning them means that we no longer want to perform them, but it does not mean that they disappear from our vital horizon. On the contrary, they are now part of our personal history, determining our present and future by reminding us of the paths of action which, for whatever reason, we no longer want to pursue. This reasoning, which according to Ortega not only applies to concrete individuals but can be extended to nations as collectives, is what led Ortega to conclude that man has no nature but history. This is why *my life* (each one's) can only be apprehended narratively, through the past—that is, biographically. In Ortega's words:

> Alongside pure physico-mathematical reason there is, then, a narrative reason. To comprehend anything human, be it personal or collective, one must tell its history. This man, this nation does such a thing and is in such a manner, *because* formerly he or it did that other thing and was in such another manner. Life only takes on a measure of transparency in the light of *historical reason*. [...] Here, then, awaiting our study, lies man's authentic "being"—stretching the whole length of his past. Man is what has happened to him, what he has done. Other things might have happened to him or have been done by him, but what did in fact happen to him and was done by him, this constitutes a relentless trajectory of experiences that he carries on his back as the vagabond his bundle of all he possesses. Man is a substantial emigrant on a pilgrimage of being, and it is accordingly meaningless to set limits to what he is capable of being. In this initial illimitableness of possibilities that characterizes one who has no nature there stands out only one fixed, pre-established, and given line by which he may chart his course, only one limit: the past. The experiments already made with life narrow man's future. If we do not know what he is going to be, we know what he is not going to be. Man lives in view of the past. *Man, in a word, has no nature; what he has is... history.* (Ortega y Gasset 1935a, pp. 214 *and* 216–217, author's emphasis [Ortega y Gasset 1935b, pp. 40 *and* 41])

3.2   Julián Marías: The Empirical Structure of Human Life

The subject matter of Marías's Metaphysical Anthropology is the study of the realisation of *human life* in the form of *man*. Marías's argumentation is grounded in the distinction between *my life* ("*mi vida*"), *human life* ("*vida humana*") and *man* ("*hombre*"). The precise meaning of Marías's argumentation will become clearer as this section develops, but it is crucial to begin by clearly distinguishing between these three terms to correctly comprehend Marías's Metaphysical Anthropology.

In Marías's terminology, as in Ortega's, *my life* refers to the *radical reality*, meaning that it is not a thing but the "where" in which all reality is *radicated* (in the sense of being rooted in it). *Human life* is an abstract notion that refers to biographical or personal life regardless of its concretion as *this* or *that* life—so it comprises *my life* and also each one's *life*. *Man* refers to the realisation of *human life* in the form of mankind. For reasons that will become clear later, Marías uses *man* as referring to both sexes, while using the terms "male" ("*varón*") and "woman" ("*mujer*") when wanting to make a clear distinction between them. *My life* is the subject matter of Metaphysics, while *man* is the subject matter of Anthropology. Marías named his position as Metaphysical Anthropology because the apprehension of the determinations that are constitutive of the realisation of *human life* in the form of *man*—the concretisation of what Marías named as the *empirical structure of human life* ("*estructura empírica de la vida humana*"), and whose knowledge is obtained empirically—presupposes apprehension of the necessary conditions without which there is no *human life*—what Marías named as the *analytical structure of human life* ("*estructura analítica de la vida humana*"), and whose knowledge is obtained through metaphysical analysis of *my life*.

Having made these preliminary terminological clarifications, we can now begin to analyse Marías's Metaphysical Anthropology in greater detail. As already mentioned, the starting point of Marías's argumentation is his acceptance of Ortega's ontological claim that *my life* is the *radical reality*. By claiming that *my life* is the *radical reality* Marías meant exactly the same as Ortega. *My life* is the "where" in which all *things* make themselves present. It is therefore the most fundamental reality and so it is irreducible to any one thing. Whatever reality I encounter are *things* whose reality is *radicated* (rooted) in *my life*, which is why Marías named them as "*radicated realities*" ("*realidades radicadas*"). Moreover, *my life* is not a thing or an entity. It consists in my engaging with and relating to the world I happen to coexist with—in short, in *living*. Since *my life* is not a thing but "a task" ("*un quehacer*"), it cannot be apprehended by means of description or definition but only narratively, through telling my own biography—that is, explaining what I did and how I dealt with my circumstance. In Marías's words:

> The primary meaning of the expression "life" appears when each of us speaks of his own; that is, when it is a question of *my* life. This life, and only this one, is what Ortega called *radical reality*, in the sense that it is the root of all the others, those which are to be constituted and appear in its ambit or area. My life is what I do and what happens to me; I with things, making something with them, *living*. My life is a gerund. All reality *qua* reality—as it is encountered by me in any mode whatever—springs from my life, is rooted in it. In that sense, my life contains all reality, but not in the form that reality is its content or one of its elements; rather, in the concrete form of radication, which does not even exclude the fact that that reality rooted in my life may transcend it. The analysis of my life is metaphysics insofar as what must appear in it is what we might call the "place" or mode of radication of all reality as such. (Marías 1970a, p. 49, author's emphasis [Marías 1970b, p. 61])[7]

The notion of *human life* refers to biographical or personal life regardless of its concrete realisation as *this* or *that* life. *Human life* cannot be identified with *my life*. Rather, it is a theory, an interpretation of *my life*

---

[7] See also: "Ortega's expression 'radical reality' involves two significant aspects: reality on this side (or the other) of all theory and reality in which all other realities have their *root* (radicated realities). These two aspects are inseparable. Reality is that which I find, exactly as I find it; radical reality is the 'ambit' or 'where' in which I find all reality; and it is also what is left when I eliminate all interpretations: things and I, I with things, I doing something with things, living; in short: *my life*. All reality appears to me *in my life*; this is, therefore, the ambit or area in which all reality *as reality* appears (that is, as I encounter it) no matter what that reality may be like, be it absolute, creative, or—which is more serious—impossible" (Marías 1970a, p. 53, author's emphasis [Marías 1970b, p. 65]).

obtained through metaphysical analysis. It therefore pertains to the realm of *radicated realities.* However, *human life* is not a theory like the others, but what Marías named as an "intrinsic theory". This means that it is an interpretation that I (and each one of us) must reach to apprehend what *my life* is. This is so because an intrinsic character of *my life* is that it occurs in the form of "living-with" ("*convivencia*").[8] In *my life* I encounter *radicated*, as part of my circumstance, realities of a sort that I recognise akin to *my life*, and for which I seem to appear to them as their respective circumstance. My confrontation with these other *lives* that are not *my life* is what, according to Marías, allows me (and each one of us) to apprehend *my life* as it being *mine*. *Human life* is an "intrinsic theory" because to apprehend *my life* as *mine* I must apprehend the intrinsic disjunctive character of *my life* (each one his own), which inevitably gets me to form the general and abstract notion of *human life*. Marías states his argument as follows:

> When I say that "human life" is a theory, but not a theory like the rest, what do I mean? Reality pure and simple is *my life*—each person's life. *This life* means individuality, singularity, absolute, irreducible position; "human life" is, on the other hand, an interpretation which I *must* reach. The reason for this is that my life occurs in the form of *living-with* ["*convivencia*"]; it is the concrete form which its circumstanciality presents in one of its dimensions. *In my life* I encounter *other lives*. I discover myself as an *I*, not primarily, but in confrontation with a *thou* (secondarily with a he or a she); and this is the primary meaning of the expression "*my* life". But what interests me more just now is the *disjunctive* quality (*my* life or *yours* or *his*, this *or* this *or* this life), which brings us to a new notion: "life". Let us not say "life in general" yet, for we are not dealing with a universal, a species, or a genus. *My* life, radical reality, appears to me as *this* concrete life, a circumstantial *disjunction* of "life", which is the life of *each person*. If we want to speak of universals, we shall have to say that it is a new posing of this problem, which in no wise reduces itself to the traditional one (individuals and

---

[8] As mentioned in Chap. 2, there is no straightforward English translation of the Spanish term "*convivencia*". Its usual translation is "coexistence", but "*convivencia*" is not just existing with things but living in the company of other persons. Frances M. López-Morillas, the English translator of *Antropología metafísica*, translates "*convivencia*" as "living-with". A. Robert Caponigri, the English translator of *Idea de la metafísica*, translates it as "shared living".

genuses or species). Living-with ["*convivencia*"] is *intrinsic* to my life, for the human world is *social*, composed of interpretations, and in *my* life there is *already* a reference to *other* lives, and consequently to *life* in general. But observe that the latter does not have any primary meaning, and that it is absolutely unthinkable without the intuition of *my* life. (Marías 1970a, pp. 55–56, author's emphasis [Marías 1970b, p. 68]; see also: Marías 1954a, pp. 355–358 [Marías 1954b, pp. 401–403])

The analysis of *my life* leads me to identify its *a priori* necessary conditions. These necessary conditions are found in *my life,* but given the intrinsic *living-with* character of *my life*, I infer that they are requirements not just of *my life* but of each one's life regardless of its concrete realisation as *this* or *that* life—so they apply to the general theory of *human life*. They are a priori necessary inasmuch as without them no individual biography is intelligible. They do not depend on any concrete biographical content of an individual life as that life, but rather are presupposed in any personal life. These conditions configure what Marías named as the *analytical structure of human life* ("*estructura analítica de la vida humana*"). It is named "analytical" because despite applying to the theory of *human life* these conditions are first identified through the metaphysical analysis of the *radical reality* that is *my life*. In Marías's words:

[…] the only real life is individual, *mine* (the "mine" of each man); it is singular, temporal, circumstantial, and its expression is a *telling* of it; but I cannot understand, narrate, or tell *my* life except from the structure of life per se, which does not have reality. This structure is obtained by analysis of *my* life, and consists in the repertory of its necessary *requisites*, of its conditions *sine quibus non*. The universality of this "life" interpretation arises from this necessary quality: it contains the conditions without which *there is no life*, and which, in consequence, must necessarily be given in *each* life. Hence the notion "human life" can be changed to "human life in general". […] Human life has a structure which I discover by *analysis* of *my* life. The result of that analysis is a theory which we therefore call analytical; I stress the fact that it is not a reality—the reality is *my* life, *each* life—but a theory or interpretation. But it is arrived at from reality; and its contents are the *requisites*, the conditions without which my life is not possible, and which must therefore be found in each life. It is a necessary structure and *therefore* universal; it exists *a priori* with regard to each life, but is derived from the analysis of reality and is in no wise an aprioristic construction. (Marías 1970a, pp. 60 *and* 70, author's emphasis [Marías 1970b, pp. 72 *and* 85])

The conditions that shape the *analytical structure of human life* are derived from Ortega's claim that *living* consists in engaging with and relating to the world I happen to coexist with—"I am myself and my circumstance" (*"Yo soy yo y mi circumtancia"*). *My life* (and each one's) is not, therefore, a substantial, metaphysical entity but rather "an activity" (*"un quehacer"*). It is biographical, in the sense that it cannot be apprehended by means of description or definition but only narratively, through telling my own biography. Living consists in personalising the world by projecting onto it my own vital project, what Marías named as "vocation" (*"vocación"*), explaining his claim that life is constitutively "projective" (*"proyectiva"*)—and so also "futureward" (*"futuriza"*) and requiring of imagination, since projecting ultimately refers to the future. In Marías's words:

> That necessary structure which the analytical theory discovers could therefore be called *analytical structure* of human life. Its maximum condensation would be Ortega's thesis of 1914: *I am I and my circumstance*. Its explication would demonstrate the metaphysical doctrine which I have explained in other books: the circumstance as stage setting or world [...]; the "I" as a *who*, a project, pretension, or vital program; the circumstance as repertory of facilities or difficulties, which become possibilities (or impossibilities) when my projects are projected upon them; the nature, at once plural and limited, of that "keyboard" of possibilities; the need to *do* something with things in order to live, to decide or choose (pre-fer), possible by means of justification in virtue of a "why" or a "wherefore" which requires "giving a reason"—vital reason. (Marías 1970a, p. 71, author's emphasis [Marías 1970b, p. 86])

The *analytical structure of human life* is an abstract interpretation of *my life,* which lacks concreteness. I find it through the analysis of *my life,* which is a concrete reality. However, it does not amount to a narration of *my life,* nor of any other concrete individual *human life*. Rather, and as previously explained, it refers to the necessary requisites without which there is no *human life*—necessary because without their presupposition no biography is intelligible. In Marías's expression, the conditions referred to in the *analytical structure of human life* resemble the "empty places" of algebraic formulas. These formulas are the necessary instruments for us to gain concrete knowledge, but they are not themselves concrete knowledge. It is not until the blanks are "filled" that these algebraic formulas allow us to gain concrete knowledge. The conditions referred to in the *analytical structure of human life* are the so to say "empty places" of a concrete biography: they are the necessary presuppositions for telling or narrating a concrete individual *human life* (and so to get apprehension of it), but they are not by themselves knowledge of any individual and concrete *human life*. In Marías's words:

> These analytical structures permit us to apprehend the singular reality of *each* life; for example, to *narrate* it. The narration of the individual life is possible by means of universal structures, which in each case are gradually fleshed out with circumstantial concretion. They are—to use Ortega's expression—*leere Stellen*, "empty places", like an algebraic formula destined to be "filled in" or fulfilled by acquiring numerical values. The formula is not yet knowledge, nor is knowledge possible without the formula. In like manner, analytical theory is not yet *real* knowledge—it is only knowledge of an unreal structure—but concrete reality is graspable only by means of that theory. The decisive point is that those structures are *previous* to each individual life, but they are *given*; their character is not speculative; rather, they are given in the true, individual reality which is my life, from which they are obtained by analysis. (Marías 1970a, p. 72, author's emphasis [Marías 1970b, p. 87])

The *analytical structure of human life* is not, however, the only necessary presupposition we need to make to apprehend a concrete individual *human life*. The fact is that we find *human life* realised in the form of what we call *man*. Being a *man* implies certain constitutive determinations. They are constitutive inasmuch as they are presupposed in the biography of each concrete *man,* while they are independent of the biographical content of a *man* as that concrete *man* and not another. To apprehend a *human life* that occurs in its realisation as *man*, we need apprehension of these constitutive conditions. They are not referred to in the *analytical structure of human life* so they are not grounded in the *a priori* require-ments for any *human life*. This means that the fact that we only find *human life* realised in the form of *man* is an empirical contingent fact. According to Marías's schema, once the requirements referred to in the *analytical structure of human life* are met, there is no *a priori* reason for denying that *human life*, in the sense of personal or biographical life, may be realised in other forms distinct from the reality of *man*. However, the point remains that to apprehend an individual *human life* in its concrete realisation as *man*, we need apprehension of the constitutive and presup-posed conditions of what being a *man* are.

Consider the following example. Suppose we are trying to apprehend an individual *human life*. Since it is not an object but a personal reality, it cannot be apprehended by means of description or definition, but only narratively—so we need to discover what he or she did, his or her biogra-phy. Now, suppose we find a biographical tale telling of that individual *human life*. So we are told that her name was Calliope, that she was born on such a date and in such a place, and that she did such and such. Now, suppose that at one point in Calliope's biography, we are told that Calliope became pregnant by Octavius. This statement presupposes that Calliope was a woman, that Octavius was a male, and that at some point they both engaged in a very precise kind of physical relationship, which resulted in Calliope's pregnancy. This content of the biography of Calliope is unin-telligible without *prior* understanding of three *facts*: first, that the reality of *man* is concreted in the disjunction of being either a male or a female; second, that a male and a woman can engage in a particular and very precise kind of physical relationship that we name "coitus" and which has a procreative function; third, that the woman but not the male may get pregnant. Understanding these facts cannot be derived from the concrete content of the biography of Calliope, but rather they are *presupposed* in it. There is, however, not the slightest reference to male, woman, coitus or pregnancy in the *analytical structure of human life*. The claim that "I am myself and my circumstance" ("*Yo soy yo y mi circunstancia*") is silent regarding the fact that *human life*, as we encounter it in the reality of *man*, is concreted in the form of being either a male or a woman, or in the kind of relationships that can occur between them—and so our apprehension of these presuppositions cannot be derived from the metaphysical analysis of *my life*, meaning that they are not *a priori* require-ments for any *human life*. To apprehend an individual *human life*, it is therefore necessary to make more presuppositions than just the *analytical structure of human life*. Since they are not a priori requirements for *human life*, but are nonetheless presupposed in any *human life* that occurs in the form of *man*, these assumptions should be considered as the constitutive conditions of the reality *man*—that is, they are the determinations that distinguish the reality of *man* from other forms in which *human life* may be, at least in principle, realisable. In *Antropología metafísica*, Marías makes this point using the example of a dictionary entry on the Spanish writer Miguel de Cervantes:

[…] when it [the dictionary] speaks of Cervantes it offers us a narration; it tells us where and when he was born, where he travelled to, where he lived, whom he married, what he wrote, where and when he died. Now, what are the assumptions of that article in the dictionary? When we read the proper, the "personal" name of Cervantes, we think that he is a man, and this refers us to a particular reality; whatever is said of Cervantes *presupposes* the ana-lytical theory of human life, which is functioning tacitly all the while in order to make him intelligible. This is true, but insufficient; it is truth, but not the whole truth. In addition to the analytical or general theory of human life, in order to make a concrete biography intelligible, a whole other series of assumptions is interposed; they are those which constitute what we call "man". The Spanish dictionary says, for example, that Cervantes was left "*manco*" ["one-armed"] at the battle of Lepanto; but what does this word mean? It means that he lost either the use of an arm or the arm itself. And then we say, "Ah! so Cervantes had arms". The analytical theory of human life certainly does not say anything about arms, which are not an ingredient of human life in general. The dictionary, when it says that he lost the use of an arm, assumes that he had arms; therefore the dictionary makes an assumption which is not analytical theory. It also says that he married Catalina de Palacios; hence, Cervantes was a male and could have a very precise relationship with a woman named Catalina; but do we find in analytical theory the last reference to "male", "woman", "sex", "marry", etc.? No. And when the dictionary adds that Cervantes, in his old age, wrote the *Persiles*, this also goes beyond the general theory of human life, in which nothing can be said of ages and growing old. (Marías 1970a, pp. 73–74, author's emphasis [Marías 1970b, pp. 88–89]; see also: Marías 1952b [Marías 1952a])

Marías uses the term *empirical structure of human life* ("*estructura empírica de la vida humana*") to refer to the conditions that are constitutively necessary of a concrete realisation of *human life* (which is why Marías names it "structure"), despite this necessity not being grounded in any *a priori* metaphysical claim but in the way in which we empirically find that *human life* contingently happens to occur in that concrete form (which is why Marías called it "empirical"). The *empirical structure of human life* is shaped by what Marías named *installations* ("*instalaciones*"), since they determine the way in which the subject perceives and relates to the world, thereby recalling the way in which the subject is "installed" in his *own* world. In the concrete realisation of *human life* in the form of *man*, Marías identifies various *installations* such as life stages (childhood, puberty, youth, adulthood and old age), sexuate condition (being either a male or a woman), happiness, corporeity, language and being in love. These *installations* configure the common determinations which, despite not being a priori requirements, are constitutive of being a *man*. Accordingly, there is nothing incoherent in claiming that *human life* may have taken other forms, but the fact remains that the reality *man* appears to occur in this way and not in another. In Marías's words:

> Empirical structure is not, therefore, a *requisite*—or a combination of requisites—of human life, *a priori* in regard to each possible life. But it belongs to the human lives in which I discover it *empirically*. Not only in fact, but furthermore in a *stable* manner—which does not, however, mean that it is permanent. Because this is so, a certain apriorism is also a property of empirical structure, not in respect to each one of the *possible* lives, but in respect to the many *real* lives that I encounter in my experience. Human life is *like that*, though in principle it might not be. And the expression "like that" does not have a mere factual character, but a structural and configurative one. And this means that *life*, in addition to having the analytical and universal structure constituted by its necessary requisites, *sine quibus non*, must be empirically structured, with one empirical structure or another. But this means that empirical structure, taken overall, is *one* ingredient or requisite of the analytical structure of human life. Seen from this perspective, empirical structure appears as the field of *possible human variation in history*. Analytical and necessary structure is in fact articulated into stable and lasting, but in principle variable, forms in which it is realized.

And this empirical structure in its turn acquires the ultimate circumstantial and individual reality, the absolutely concrete reality, of *each* life, which *happens* dramatically, in respect to which the possible and adequate form of "enunciation" is to *narrate it*. (Marías 1970a, pp. 75–76, author's emphasis [Marías 1970b, p. 91])

The following example will clarify the point, while also explaining why in Marías's terminology the term *man* refers to both male and woman. The disjunctive fact of being either a male or a woman—what Marías named as the "sexuate condition" ("*condición sexuada*")—is an *installation*, and so pertains to the *empirical structure of human life* as we find it concreted in *man*. It is, therefore, an empirically constitutive determination of the realisation of *human life* in the form of *man*, but it is not an a priori requirement for *human life* as such. This means that there is no *man* that is not concreted as being either a male or a woman (despite the varying ways in which each concrete *man* is installed in his or her own sexuate condition). However, in principle it is still coherent to claim the existence of a non-sexuate *human life*—but that this non-sexuate life will not be a *man*.

Marías's analysis on the debate at the popular level on the possibility of extraterrestrial life is worth commenting on since it succeeds in intuitively illustrating the distinction between *human life* and *man*—and therefore also between the *analytical structure of human life* and the *empirical structure of human life*. The fact is that *man* is the only kind of *human life* known to us. However, this is just an empirically contingent fact, meaning that even if we had enough reasons to conclude that it is improbable, it should still be granted that it is conceptually possible that there is *human life* that is not concretised in the form of *man*—provided that the requirements referred to in the *analytical structure of human life* are met. Now, Marías points out that this is precisely what underpins the debate on the possibility of extraterrestrial life as it is discussed by non-scientific people and in popular culture. When thinking of the possibility that there may be extraterrestrial life, common people are not asking whether there may be biological life apart from that on planet Earth—everybody of course agrees that the discovery of microorganisms on any planet that is not ours would be of scientific interest, but this would not answer the question of whether there is or not extraterrestrial life as it is popularly framed. Neither is it a question of finding beings that are somehow "intelligent"—after all, artificial intelligence is, in a relevant sense, intelligence without thereby being life. Rather, and again on a popular level, the question is ultimately whether outside our planet there is *human life* in the sense of personal or biographical life that is different from *man*. In other words, whether there is *human life* but with an *empirical structure* other than that of *man*. Notice that this is the common way in which extraterrestrial beings are displayed in popular culture and in most sci-fi fictions. To give a concrete example that will be easily recognisable to all readers, think about how extraterrestrials are represented in movies such as *Star Wars* or *Men in Black*: despite resembling *man* in their intellectual abilities and, above all, in having their own biography, it is obvious that we cannot consider them as *man*. In Marías's words:

> If man, when he arrives on another planet, finds no life or finds only "biological" life—plants, animals—he will undoubtedly feel disappointed; apparently, he desired or hope to find men. But if he finds men he will also feel cheated, and will think that he hardly needed to travel so far to find them. What does he anticipate and hope for, then? For me there is no doubt: "Life"—biographical life, personal life, of course—but with a different empirical structure. That is, what we call "human life"—because we have no intuition of any other kind—but not "men". (Marías 1970a, p. 78 [Marías 1970b, p. 94]; see also: Marías 1956)

As already mentioned, the *empirical structure of human life* is shaped by what Marías named as "installations". They are the "where" or the ambit, understood in a biographical and not a spatial sense, from which I (each one) project myself onto the world. To put it more precisely, this is tantamount to claiming that *my living*, my dealing with the circumstance with the aim of projecting onto it my own vital project, is *radicated* in the concrete way I am installed:

> *From* these different forms of life, from these biographical structures of installation, based on them, man advances in different directions, *does* what he has planned, deploys the dramatic dynamism which we call living. The

mere "circumstantiality" of human life is not enough. It is not sufficient to say that man "is in the world": we must see *how* he is in it, how he has to be or may be in it. Now we can understand the most important point, the point that would not have been fully intelligible before: installation is the empirical form of radication in human life as radical reality. (Marías 1970a, p. 88, author's emphasis [Marías 1970b, pp. 105–106])

According to Marías, then, the concrete way in which I am installed is the *radical* basis. Therefore, *how* I am installed shapes my *living*, the way I relate both theoretically and practically to my circumstance—"When I project and execute my projects—and in particular the unitary project which *I* am at each instant—I am 'leaning' on that installation, I am putting into play the ingredients which compose its structure in the precise form in which they compose it" (Marías 1970a, p. 84 [Marías 1970b, p. 101]). In short, the whole reality is lived *from* my installation. Note that this has the merit of preserving the intuitive everyday claim that living is different if you are a male or a woman, if you are a teenager or an adult, if you are in love or not, if you are happy or not, and so on with the rest of the *installations* that Marías identifies. Marías makes this point clear in the following quote from *Antropología metafísica*—the quote refers to the sexuate condition as a particular installation, but the claim that the experiential reality is different depending on *how* one is installed can be extended to the rest of the *installations* that Marías identifies:

The sexuate condition, because it is an installation, pervades, permeates, and encompasses all of life, which is lived without exception from the disjunction into man ["*varón*": "male"] and woman. All realities, even those most remote from sexuality—eating, comprehension of a mathematical theorem, contemplation of a landscape, a religious action, the experience of danger—are lived out of installation in sex, and therefore within a context and from a perspective which cannot be reduced to the other. If a professor of mathematics explains Pythagoras's theorem—and nothing could possibly be more "asexual"—the experiential reality is different according to whether he is teaching boys or girls or a mixed class. The theorem and its intellection have a sexuate significance, as they form part of the sexes' respective installation, no matter how asexual the content or object of these experiences may be. (Marías 1970a, pp. 138–139 [Marías 1970b, pp. 164–165])

Installation is multidimensional, inasmuch as it comprises different determinations which can be identified separately. As already mentioned, in the case of *human life* as it is concretised in the form of *man*, the most interesting of these installations being life stages, the sexuate condition (the fact of being either a male or a woman), happiness (not just feeling happiness but being *in* happiness), corporeity, language, and being in love. However, installation is nonetheless unitary, inasmuch as I find myself "installed" on the whole in such a way and not in another (Marías 1970a, p. 83 [Marías 1970b, p. 101]). Moreover, the claim that *human life* possesses installation is part of the *analytical structure of human life*, and so according to Marías is one of the a priori requirements without which there cannot be *human life*. This is so because the very notion of projecting presupposes that there is a "where" in which I am and from which I project myself.[9] However, the fact that an individual *human life* possesses such or such a kind of installation is not an analytical but an empirical claim—and so pertains to the *empirical structure of human life*. Therefore, the study of installations in the realisation of *human life* in the form of *man* is not the task of Metaphysics, but of Anthropology:

> Now one feature of the analytical structure is that human life possesses installation, and that is the only thing which the general theory of human life knows. Just *what* this installation may be is something that belongs to empirical structure, and therefore knowledge of it is accessible only to anthropology. (Marías 1970a, p. 84, author's emphasis [Marías 1970b, p. 102])

Therefore, according to Marías, living, my dealing with my circumstance, does not arise from the void but is *radicated* in the concrete way I (and each one of us) are installed. Moreover, living is not directionless. Living is not just doing but doing with the attempt to realise my own vocation or vital project—that is, projecting. This is why living refers to

---

[9] See: "I can only project—and this means project myself—from what I was *already* doing, from that 'in which' I already was. We could say that no human project is 'primary' or initial, or, in other words, that human life never starts off from zero. This is what I call *installation*. I cannot live in a forward direction except *out of* a previous manner of being—previous in respect to *each* project and each thing I do—in which I am 'installed'" (Marías 1970a, p. 83, author's emphasis [Marías 1970b, p. 100]).

the future—it is constitutively *"futurizo"* ("futureward").[10] Taken altogether, this means that *human life* has a "vectorial structure". By living, the things of the world—that is, my circumstance—become integrated in this vectorial structure—meaning that they become interconnected with both the concrete way I am installed and with my own vital project. This interconnection gives things a significance *for me*—that is, things take on a biographical significance, related to my own biography and so independent of the significance they could have in themselves, regardless of my relation to them. In Marías's expression, things take a "slant" (*"sesgo"*)—accordingly, "slant" can be defined as "[…] the manner of being of things when they are realities lived from a vectorial structure" (Marías 1970a, p. 96 [Marías 1970b, p. 114]). In Marías's words:

> Man—not his body, not man considered as an organism—needs many things in order to live, and is connected with them through a system of projects, tensions, memories, anticipations, deprivations, which have intensity and orientation; that is, a vectorial character. Within each life, things are arranged in a rigorous and shifting perspective; they assume different functions or roles, they are arranged in a precise hierarchy whose principle is internal to that life and does not coincide with the hierarchy that external consideration would suppose. Those two concepts of "intensity" and "directedness" characteristic of the vector become in the biographical sphere "importance" and "significance", or, if you prefer, "meaning". Things "carry me along" according to their importance, and in a direction determined by the meaning they have form me, by their significance—this is why life is interpretation of itself and of its contents. (Marías 1970a, p. 93 [Marías 1970b, pp. 110–111])

The claim that *human life* has a vectorial structure is a necessary requirement, and as such it pertains to the *analytical structure of human life*—as already explained, it is inferred from the a priori necessary requirements that any *human life* has an *installation* (regardless of how

---

[10] See: "The *executive* I, the true I in its pronominal function—not the substantive one, not 'the I'—the function in which I say 'I', is present, is pure presentness and momentness, but its reality consists in projecting itself vectorially toward the future. *I* am not future, but present and actual and acting, and therefore *future-oriented*" (Marías 1970a, p. 212, author's emphasis [Marías 1970b, p. 248]).

this installation is concretised) and that *living* is a directed movement aimed at realising my (each one's) vocation or vital programme (regardless of what this vocation consists of). However, the concrete way in which this vectorial structure is realised in each individual *human life* is found empirically, by apprehension of each one's concrete biography. It is therefore a conceptual, metaphysical claim that living gives a personal or biographical significance to the world—which means that by living, *the* world becomes *my* (each one his own) world:

> [...] for man, "to be located" is "to be living"; to be in the world means to be *making* the world, to be "worldifying". Man is certainly not a creator, and therefore he "finds himself" in the world, but he is a demiurge. He makes the world—"his" world—with that which is given to him but which until then is only circumstance. "The reabsorption of the circumstance is the concrete destiny of man", wrote Ortega in *Meditations on Quixote*, and I have analyzed this decisive text minutely. (Marías 1970a, p. 105 [Marías 1970b, p. 125])

References

Marías, J. (1952a) 1971. Human Life and its Empirical Structure. In *Philosophy as Dramatic Theory*, trans. James Parsons, 131–140. Pennsylvania: The Pennsylvania State University Press.

Marías, J. (1952b) 1959. La vida humana y su estructura empírica. In *Julián Marías: Obras (vol. IV)*, 341–347. Madrid: Revista de Occidente.

Marías, J. (1954a) 1967. The Idea of Metaphysics. In *Contemporary Spanish Philosophy: An Anthology*, trans. and ed. A. Robert Caponigri, 324–370. Notre Dame: University of Notre Dame Press.

Marías, J. (1954b) 1962. Idea de la metafísica. In *Julián Marías: Obras (vol. II)*, 369–413. Madrid: Revista de Occidente.

Marías, J. (1956) 1958. Los otros mundos. In Julián Marías, *El oficio del pensamiento*, 167–173. Madrid: Biblioteca Nueva.

Marías, J. (1970a) 1971. *Metaphysical Anthropology: The Empirical Structure of Human Life*. Trans. Frances M. López-Morillas. Pennsylvania: The Pennsylvania State University Press.

Marías, J. (1970b). *Antropología metafísica: la estructura empírica de la vida humana*. Madrid: Revista de Occidente.

Marías, J. (1971). *Philosophy as Dramatic Theory*. Trans. James Parsons. Pennsylvania: The Pennsylvania State University Press.

Ortega y Gasset, J. (1914a) 1961. *Meditations on Quixote*. Trans. Evelyn Rugg and Diego Marín. New York: W. W. Norton & Company.

Ortega y Gasset, J. (1914b) 1946. Meditaciones del Quijote. In *José Ortega y Gasset: Obras Completas (vol. I: 1902–1916)*, 309–400. Madrid: Revista de Occidente.

Ortega y Gasset, J. (1922a) 1974. *Invertebrate Spain*. Trans. Mildred Adams. New York: Howard Fertig.

Ortega y Gasset, J. (1922b) 1947. España invertebrada. In *José Ortega y Gasset: Obras Completas (vol. III: 1917–1928)*, 35–128. Madrid: Revista de Occidente.

Ortega y Gasset, J. (1923a) 1961. *The Modern Theme*. Trans. James Cleugh. New York: Harper & Row Publishers.

Ortega y Gasset, J. (1923b) 1947. El tema de nuestro tiempo. In *José Ortega y Gasset: Obras Completas (vol. III: 1917–1928)*, 141–242. Madrid: Revista de Occidente.

Ortega y Gasset, J. (1929a) 1932. *The Revolt of the Masses*. New York: W. W. Norton & Company.

Ortega y Gasset, J. (1929b) 1947. La rebelión de las masas. In *José Ortega y Gasset: Obras Completas (vol. IV: 1929–1933)*, 111–310. Madrid: Revista de Occidente.

Ortega y Gasset, J. (1935a) 1961. History as a System. In José Ortega y Gasset, *History as a System and Other Essays Toward a Philosophy of History*, trans. Helene Weyl, 165–233. New York: W. W. Norton & Company.

Ortega y Gasset, J. (1935b) 1947. Historia como sistema. In *José Ortega y Gasset: Obras Completas (vol. VI: 1941–1946)*, 11–50. Madrid: Revista de Occidente.

Ortega y Gasset, J. (1957a) 1964. *What is Philosophy?*. Trans. Mildred Adams. New York: W. W. Norton & Company.

Ortega y Gasset, J. (1957b) 1961. ¿Qué es filosofía?. In *José Ortega y Gasset: Obras Completas (vol. VII: 1948–1958)*, 273–438. Madrid: Revista de Occidente.

Ortega y Gasset, J. (1957c) 1963. *Man and People*. Trans. Willard R. Trask. New York: W. W. Norton & Company.

Ortega y Gasset, J. (1957d) 1961. El hombre y la gente. In *José Ortega y Gasset: Obras Completas (vol. VII: 1948–1958)*, 69–269. Madrid: Revista de Occidente.

4

Julián Marías on Human Happiness, Death and the Call for Personal Immortality

Abstract This chapter discusses Marías's argumentation for affirming that *my life* (each one's) presupposes, not as an epistemic attitude of part of I myself, the executive I, but as an intrinsic ontological postulate without which *my life* itself as *radical reality* is *impossible*, the assumption of its own indefinite perduration. This allows Marías to conclude that my (each one's) conscious hope for personal immortality after my *biological death* occurs is justified inasmuch as it is a self-affirming exercise, a conscious endorsement of my own *human* reality, and so a sign of authenticity. Marías's argumentation is complex, composed of several argumentative steps. The crucial step in Marías's argumentation is his identification of human happiness with the realisation of living. It is argued that this identification is problematic even under Marías's premises.

Keywords Death • Human happiness • Julián Marías • Personal immortality

On the basis of his Metaphysical Anthropology, Marías formulated a conception of human happiness which, as will be explained in this chapter,

© The Author(s), under exclusive license to Springer Nature Switzerland AG 2024
A. Oya, *The Metaphysical Anthropology of Julián Marías*, Palgrave Frontiers in
Philosophy of Religion, https://doi.org/10.1007/978-3-031-61804-8_4

lead him to conclude that *my life* (each one's) presupposes, not as an epistemic attitude by part of I myself, the executive I, but as an intrinsic postulate without which *my life* itself as *radical reality* is *impossible*, the assumption of its own indefinite perduration. This allowed Marías to justify my (each one's) conscious hope for personal immortality after *biological death* inasmuch as it is a self-affirming exercise, a conscious endorsement of my own *human* reality, and so a sign of authenticity. Marías's conception of human happiness and its connection with death and the call for personal immortality is extensively developed in his book *La felicidad humana* (Marías 1987) [*The Human Happiness*], although his position in this regard had already been clearly formulated in the last chapters of *Antropología metafísica: la estructura empírica de la vida humana* (Marías 1970b) [*Metaphysical Anthropology: The Empirical Structure of Human Life* (Marías 1970a)] (hereafter referred to as *Antropología metafísica*). Marías's first approach to the topic of human happiness can be traced back to as early as 1952, in his essay "La felicidad humana: mundo y paraíso" (Marías 1952b) ["Human Happiness: The World and Paradise" (Marías 1952a)].

According to Marías, and as already explained in detail in Chap. 3, *my life* (each one's) is the *radical reality*, meaning that it is the fundamental reality—whatever reality I encounter are *things* whose reality is *radicated* ("rooted") in *my life*. Moreover, *my life* is not a substantial metaphysical entity but "a task" ("*un quehacer*"). This task is what we name as "living"— that is, my dealing with my circumstance, my engaging with and relating to the world I happen to coexist with. My living is not directionless but aimed at realising my own vocation or vital programme—living is, therefore, projective and so "future-oriented" ("*futuriza*"). A *human life* may be realised on different kinds of *empirical structure* provided that the a priori necessary requirements referred to in the *analytical structure of human life* are met. However, the given fact is that I find *my life* realised as the reality *man*. Whereas *man* is *what* I am, my vocation constitutes the *who* I am.

Marías identifies human happiness with the realisation of my (each one his own) vocation. Human happiness occurs, therefore, when my living aligns with my vocation. In other words, and to put it more intuitively, happiness occurs when I do what I sincerely think I should do— when I give a sincere "yes" to what I am doing. When this happens, my vocation—and so the *who* I am—becomes realised and projected into the world. In Marías's words:

> Happiness is that to which we say "yes," that with which we coincide, which we feel as our inexorable reality, without which we are not ourselves. But to bring it into existence requires the positive *response* of that which we feel as our most proper vocation; without a favorable response from the circumstance, we cannot be really, presently happy, though in all cases the imaginary trajectory of our happiness can be traced. When this happens, the expansion of our own programmatic, projective reality takes place; the vectors which make up our life, at least the "resultant" vector which is our radical vocation, reach their target. Then happiness *occurs*, it touches or affects us, fills us; when the arrows reach their goal, installation is full to running over, time seems to stop, to cease flowing, and we get a whiff of eternity, precisely because time keeps on flowing without stopping, like water in the eddy of a river. (Marías 1970a, p. 242, author's emphasis [Marías 1970b, p. 282])[1]

From this stance, human happiness is not an add-on but the fulfilment of the task of living, the realisation of our vocation and so of our projective, and therefore future-oriented, constitutive condition. A happy life is, then, a self-affirming authentic life. This explains Marías's claims such as that "[...] happiness consists primarily in the *intensity of life*" (Marías 1987, p. 66, author's emphasis),[2] "[t]o live is to be doing something that fills life" (Marías 1987, p. 172),[3] and "[...] happiness is *life itself*: when it reaches its plenitude, it is happiness" (Marías 1987, p. 254, author's emphasis).[4] In his *Antropología metafísica*, Marías is clear in that happiness

---

[1] See also: "Happiness thus consists [...] in the realization of a certain aspiration or vital project that is constructed within a repertory of definite circumstances. That is, what is involved is a certain pressure that I exert upon circumstances, circumstances which make it possible or impossible for me to realize that aspiration, project, program, or (more rigorously) vocation. If I achieve it, we say that I am happy; if I do not achieve it, we say that I am unhappy, unsuccessful, miserable, unfortunate [...]" (Marías 1952a, p. 210 [Marías 1952b, p. 370]).

[2] My translation. The original Spanish text reads: "[...] la felicidad consiste primariamente en la *intensidad de la vida*".

[3] My translation. The original Spanish text reads: "Vivir es estar haciendo algo que llena la vida".

[4] My translation. The original Spanish text reads: "[...] la felicidad es *la vida misma*: cuando alcanza su plenitud, es felicidad".

is not an add-on but the fulfilment of living: "The decisive point is that happiness is not different from the reality of human life. It might seem that one first 'is' and then is or is not happy. This is not true" (Marías 1970a, p. 243 [Marías 1970b, p. 284]). This same claim is made even more explicit in his later *La felicidad humana*:

> Lack of happiness, or the loss of happiness when there already was, means a *diminution of reality*. It is not that if you lose happiness, you live in a worse way, have less pleasure or more suffering: the serious thing is that *you are less*, you live, you think, you love from a fraction of your own reality. Such is the nature of that strange reality, incomparable to any other, which is our life. (Marías 1987, p. 255, author's emphasis)[5]

Vocation refers to the *who* ("*el quién*") that each one of us, intimately and uniquely, is called to be. According to Marías, I am not the "author" of my vocation. Rather, my vocation "is proposed to me" ("*me es propuesta*")—throughout the course of life I (and each one of us) feel the "call" to be a certain *who*. I do not decide, therefore, the content of my vocation. However, neither is my vocation "imposed on me" ("*no me es impuesta*"). While I cannot deny the fact of being called to be this *who* and not another *who*, strictly speaking there is nothing that forces me to stick to my vocation. Taking the two claims together, this means that despite not being free to choose the content of my vocation, I am nonetheless free to *decide* whether to be faithful to it. My conscious decision to be faithful to the call of the vocation that I feel is proposed to me but nonetheless is not imposed on me, amounts to a self-affirmation exercise—I freely and consciously embrace the task of realising the *who* I am called to be. In *Antropología metafísica*, Marías defines vocation as follows: "Destiny, freely accepted but not chosen—that is, I choose that it be 'my' destiny, I 'adopt' it, but I do not choose its content—is my vocation, and the reality of that vocation is what we call happiness" (Marías 1970a, p. 244 [Marías

---

[5] My translation. The original Spanish text reads: "La falta de felicidad, o su pérdida cuando la había, significa una *disminución de la realidad*. No es que si se pierde la felicidad se viva peor, se tenga menos placer o mayor sufrimiento: lo grave es que *se es menos,* se vive, se piensa, se ama desde una fracción de la propia realidad. Tal es la índole de esa extraña realidad, sin comparación con ninguna otra, que es nuestra vida".

1970b, p. 284]). In one of his later books, published in 1995 and entitled *Tratado de lo mejor: la moral y las formas de vida* (Marías 1995) [*Treatise on the Best: The Moral and the Ways of Life*], Marías offers a clearer account of his notion of vocation:

There is a *project* that constitutes the ultimate and radical argument of life: that of being a certain *someone*, an irreplaceable *who* that we feel called to be. This project is more or less explicit and articulated, it is being discovered, sometimes laboriously and with extraordinary slowness, on other occasions suddenly and like a revelation, which can be dazzling. It is frequent, and so occurs to most persons, that this project is extremely vague, barely a suspicion, a simple hint of what one "should be". The individual reaction may be one of fear, laziness, perhaps terror; the image of the project that is announced is discarded, as if it were a bad temptation, because its difficulties or risks are guessed. Another possibility is that the project presents itself with such force and evidence that it cannot be shunned or postponed: then it is embraced, it is felt that "this is what we were born for", whether it be to cultivate a discipline or to love a woman. That one is the vocation that we *are*, inexorable and non-transferable. But before it *we are free*, not free to feel and recognise it, but free to follow it or not, to realise it or abandon it. We have not chosen it—we have the impression that it has chosen us—but we have to choose between being *faithful* to it or not. The degree of reality of life depends on that faithfulness. It is on this that one ultimately makes balance, provided that the hazards of our biography allow us to make this recapitulation. (Marías 1995, p. 165, author's emphasis)[6]

---

[6] My translation. The original Spanish text reads: "Hay un *proyecto* que constituye el argumento último y radical de la vida: el de ser *alguien* determinado, un *quién* insustituible que nos sentimos llamados a ser. Ese proyecto es más o menos explícito y articulado, se va descubriendo, a veces trabajosamente y con extraordinaria lentitud, en otras ocasiones súbitamente y como una revelación, que puede ser deslumbradora. Es frecuente, y así ocurre en la mayoría de las personas, que ese proyecto sea sumamente vago, apenas una sospecha, un simple barrunto de lo que 'tendría que ser'. La reacción individual puede ser de temor, pereza, acaso terror; se desecha la imagen del proyecto que se anuncia, como si fuese una mala tentación, porque se adivinan sus dificultades o sus riesgos. Otra posibilidad es que el proyecto se presente con tal fuerza y evidencia, que no quepa rehuirlo o aplazarlo: entonces se lo acoge, se siente que 'se ha nacido para eso', sea para cultivar una disciplina o para amar a una mujer. Esa es la vocación que *somos*, inexorable e intransferible. Pero ante ella *somos libres*, no de sentirla y reconocerla, sino de seguirla o no, realizarla o abandonarla. No la hemos elegido—tenemos la impresión de que nos ha elegido ella—, pero tenemos que elegir entre serle o no *fieles*. El grado de realidad de la vida depende de esa fidelidad. De esto es de lo que últimamente se hace balance, si los azares de nuestra biografía permiten hacer esa recapitulación".

According to Marías, then, human happiness refers to the realisation of my (each one his own) personal vocation. It is important to emphasise that my vocation should not be confused with the concrete paths of acting—"trajectories", in Marías's terminology—by which I seek to realise my vocation. Provided they align with my vocation, the realisation of these trajectories will amount to the realisation of my vocation and so to the enjoyment of happiness, but the crucial point is that these trajectories are not my vocation. This is important to emphasise because first, and as will be commented on later, my vocation may be realisable in different mutually exclusive trajectories, and second, and this is what I want to comment on now, because my vocation, the *who* I am called to be, is dynamic. Throughout the course of life, my vocation, the *who* I am called to be, may vary. This means that a trajectory may have been aligned to my past vocation, but now if my vocation has changed, sticking to that same trajectory will no longer be an attempt at self-affirmation, but quite the contrary. Marías illustrates this point with the example of the middle-aged man who has lost his youthful intellectual vocation and for whom, therefore, sticking to his originary intellectual trajectory is no longer an act of personal affirmation:

> Happiness corresponds to that *who* one is, to that *someone* that each of us is. [...] But that *who* that each one of us is when we say "I" is not static; it is living, it happens, it has a history with multiple trajectories, successive and simultaneous. [...] A decisive aspect is what we might name the authentication of the project or, on the contrary, its falsification. The original project can become increasingly refined, purified, becoming more and more its own and irreplaceable. But it can also be distorted, losing reality—that is, projective reality—literally *alienating*. Let us take as an example a vocation. It is common for there to be a young person with a lively intellectual vocation, maybe philosophy, mathematics, history. He is twenty or thirty years old, and he embarks on that path, he makes that discipline his main occupation, it becomes his capital trajectory. And he builds a social self around that vocation. It may last and go on intensifying throughout life; but what can happen is that he loses it. He really did have it, but when he reaches the age of forty he is interested in other things: money, politics, that which is called "figuring" ["*figurar*"]. It is possible that he has magnificent intellectual gifts for what his initial vocation was—

perhaps he confused the gifts and the enjoyment their exercise provokes with the vocation itself—; above all, his figure, his prestige, his fame, everything is linked to it, but he no longer feels it; we would say that he is married to it, but disillusioned. Life is difficult when this hiatus between the past vocation and the present situation is produced; it is unlikely that the one concerned will recognise it, because he has the vivid memory of his past vocation, he has the gifts, and he feels the shadow of the old joy when he exercises them, but he has ceased to feel the call of that vocation, and this makes happiness difficult. (Marías 1987, pp. 275–276, author's emphasis)[7]

Human happiness is not therefore to be faithful to a concrete trajectory, but rather consists in being faithful to my (each one his own) vocation. In the previous example of the middle-aged man who has lost his youthful intellectual vocation, the problem is not his change of vocation—this can happen without implying any inauthenticity since no one is free to choose the content of his vocation—but his stubbornly sticking to a past trajectory that no longer aligns with the *who* he feels now called to be:

We go on discovering *who we are* as we do or things happen to us to which we say yes to from the depth of our person and not from convenience or

---

[7] My translation. The original Spanish text reads: "La felicidad corresponde a ese *quien* que se es, a ese *alguien* que cada uno es. […] Pero ese *quien* que es cada uno de nosotros cuando dice 'yo', no es estático; es viviente, acontece, tiene una historia con múltiples trayectorias, sucesivas y simultáneas. […] Un aspecto decisivo es lo que podríamos llamar la autentificación del proyecto o, por el contrario, su falsificación. El proyecto originario se puede ir acendrando, depurando, haciéndose cada vez más propio e insustituible. Pero igualmente puede ir desvirtuándose, perdiendo realidad—se entiende, realidad proyectiva—, irse, literalmente, *enajenando*. Tomemos como ejemplo una vocación. Es frecuente que haya un joven con viva vocación intelectual, tal vez la filosofía, la matemática, la historia. Tiene veinte o treinta años y entra en ese camino, hace de esa disciplina su ocupación principal, se va convirtiendo en su trayectoria capital. Y se construye un yo social en torno a esa vocación. Acaso perdura y se va intensificando a lo largo de toda la vida; pero puede ocurrir que se le pase. La ha tenido realmente, pero al llegar a los cuarenta años le interesan otras cosas: el dinero, la política, eso que se llama 'figurar'. Es posible que tenga magníficas dotes intelectuales para lo que fue su vocación inicial—quizás confundió las dotes y la fruición que provoca su ejercicio con la vocación misma—; sobre todo, su figura, su prestigio, su fama, todo está ligado a ella, pero ya no la siente; diríamos que está casado con ella, pero desilusionado. Es difícil la vida cuando se produce ese hiato entre la vocación pasada y la situación presente; es improbable que el interesado lo reconozca, porque tiene el recuerdo vivo de su vocación pretérita, tiene las dotes, y siente como la sombra del goce antiguo cuando las ejercita, pero ha dejado de sentir la llamada de esa vocación, y esto hace difícil la felicidad".

from the current objective estimation or mere taste. When that "yes" is said from our ultimate depth, that is the sign of authenticity. But there is still another condition needed, and that is that we simultaneously say *yes* to that depth of ours, that itself is authentic. In the previous example, the person defined by his old intellectual vocation, deep down no longer says *yes* to it and is eager to say goodbye to it; but he does not solidarise with that depth of his, he does not make it his own, and the possible new authenticity escapes him. What is needed is the double simultaneous "yes" to the content of the trajectory and to the depth from which the first "yes" is said. (Marías 1987, p. 276, author's emphasis)[8]

Neither should human happiness be confused with the circumstantial conditions that may make the realisation of my vocation (each one his own) more or less favourable. Living consists in my doing with things, in my projecting myself onto the world—and so it necessarily involves the world, the circumstance I happen to coexist with. Nonetheless, human happiness is still strictly speaking an exclusively personal issue, referring to the realisation of *my* (each one his own) vocation no matter what my circumstance is. This explains Marías's rejection in *La felicidad humana* of the utilitarian identification of human happiness with the so-called welfare state ("*estado del bienestar*")—that is, the reduction of happiness to the fulfilment of a set of impersonal, statistically quantifiable conditions, which (arguably) make of living something more comfortable (see: Marías 1987, pp. 145–169). Marías of course does not deny that a certain degree of well-being and comfort may favour human happiness, since it is obvious that the realisation of one's own personal vocation may be easier if one enjoys of certain favourable circumstantial conditions. However, this does not mean that human happiness is to be identified with these circumstantial conditions. After all, one can (and *should*) be

---

[8] My translation. The original Spanish text reads: "Vamos descubriendo *quiénes somos* a medida que hacemos o nos pasan cosas a las que decimos sí desde el fondo de nuestra persona y no desde la conveniencia o la estimación objetiva vigente o el mero gusto. Cuando ese 'sí' lo decimos desde nuestro fondo último, ese es el signo de autenticidad. Pero todavía hace falta otra condición, y es que a ese fondo le digamos simultáneamente *sí*, que él mismo sea auténtico. En el ejemplo anterior, la persona definida por su vocación intelectual antigua, en el fondo ya no le dice *sí* y está deseando despedirse de ella; pero no se solidariza tampoco con ese fondo, no lo hace suyo, y se le escapa la posible nueva autenticidad. Hace falta el doble 'sí' simultáneo al contenido de la trayectoria y al fondo personal desde el cual se dice el primer 'sí'".

faithful to his own vocation no matter what his circumstance is. This is precisely the mark of an authentic, self-governing life—that is, to be faithful to the *who* I am called to be no matter the whims of the circumstance. While in *La felicidad humana* Marías formulates the claim that human happiness should not be confused with any circumstantial condition primarily as a criticism of utilitarian conceptions of human happiness, in *Antropología metafísica* this same point is made in more general terms in relation to the notion of "chance" ("*azar*"). Living is choosing what I am going to do, how I am going to deal with my circumstance, but I cannot choose my circumstance—it is given, and this is what introduces chance in my living. However, while I cannot determine my circumstance, I am still able to choose how to respond to it—meaning that even given the most unfavourable circumstance, I still have the opportunity to reaffirm myself in my own vocation:

> It might be thought that chance alters the shape of human life, that it keeps life from being "ours". This is true to a certain degree, and it must be recognized that chance, still more than the pressure of things, imposes an element of strange "passivity" on life, reduces its character to an inventive and personal time. But *the configuration of chance* in each life is no less obvious. Each life, through the system of its projects, works out chance, "digests" it, incorporates it to a *form* of life. We make *our* life with chance. This becomes clear if we realize that chance itself—the very content of chance—acquires completely different biographical meanings in each of the lives which it affects. Each chance occurrence, when it lodges in a vital trajectory—or, more precisely, in a quiverful of possible trajectories— undergoes a change which consists in its personalization. We might say that chance—as a particular form of causality, or rather as "coincidence" or "instance"—becomes "my" chance, and I react to it *in my own way*; that is, personally. The style in which a biography consists is imposed on its external or adventitious contents and assimilates them to it. There has been a great deal of discussion—too much—about "adaptation to the environment". Rather, we would have to speak of "adoption of the environment", even of its chance ingredients, of the appropriation or "reabsorption" of *all* circumstance. [...] Destiny has to be adopted, accepted, appropriated, made "mine". It is not an object of choice, but it must be chosen; only thus is it a rigorously personal destiny, or, under another name, a *vocation*.

Strictly speaking, I never feel more "I"—I myself—than in the presence of a chance content which bursts into my life, when I react to it in a way that springs from the root of my person; when I discover in it the *destiny which is not chosen* and choose to make it mine, to be faithful to it; in other words, *I choose to be that unchoosable chance.* (Marías 1970a, pp. 223–225, author's emphasis [Marías 1970b, pp. 260–262])

Moreover, although human happiness is accompanied by a certain pleasing feeling of satisfaction, it should not be confused with pleasure or with any other feeling or mood. Rather, human happiness is what in Marías's terminology is named as an *installation*. As explained in Chap. 3, this means that human happiness shapes the concrete way in which I *live* my whole reality—that is, the way I perceive and project myself onto the circumstance. In Marías's words:

Happiness is always installation: when I am happy, I feel that I am "in" happiness. […] Happiness, in this world—and, I believe, in the next world as well—must be dramatic and plot-like; not a "state", but an installation from which one projects vectorially. That is why I said that happiness *occurs*; it is not simply "there" nor is one in it, nor, strictly speaking, can one "be" happy, but one is *in a state of being happy*, especially when one is about to be happy. (Marías 1970a, pp. 241 *and* 243, author's emphasis [Marías 1970b, pp. 281 *and* 283])

Marías's conceiving of human happiness as an installation succeeds in preserving the familiar, but not for that less important fact, that when one *is* happy, things in the world and what we do with them take on a new significance for us. Happiness affects my living as a whole. No matter what the external or social significance of my activities are supposed to be, or how trivial and disconnected from my vocation they may appear, when I am happy, they appear to me in a different light. As when one is in love, which is also an installation in Marías's sense (see, e.g., Marías 1970a, pp. 182–183 [Marías 1970b, pp. 214–216]), being happy, or on the contrary being unhappy, bestows upon the whole reality a personal "slant" ("*sesgo*"):

Happiness can originate in a concrete circumstance; it is born, is reported, sometimes it manifests itself in a very particular point, but it involves the totality of life and operates a transformation upon it. When a person is happy, and in the measure that he is happy, his whole life is transfigured, transformed, things acquire a new meaning which they do not have for the one who no longer possesses happiness or who has not reached it. In a privative way, unhappiness also transforms the totality of life, it puts it in another light, it establishes a different hierarchy between things: those things that seemed important cease to be important, others move to the fore. The overall equilibrium is altered, the configuration of life is transformed, the effects are not limited to the originary point. [...] If a person is happy in a certain dimension or activity, that originally happy vector appears within the beam of others, flows over them and puts them in a new light, with a different tonality. That is why trivial occupations, in themselves unrelated to happiness, are transformed when one is happy. [...] [W]e do a thousand trivial things and they have nothing to do with happiness, but if we are happy, these occupations are transfigured and acquire a kind of aureole. (Marías 1987, p. 247)[9]

According to Marías, human happiness therefore consists in the realisation of my (each one his own) vocation. It should not be confused with the concrete trajectories in which I seek to realise my vocation, nor with the circumstantial conditions that may favour its realisation. Moreover, despite human happiness being accompanied by a certain pleasant feeling of satisfaction, it is not a feeling or mood but an installation in Marías's terminology.

---

[9] My translation. The original Spanish text reads: "La felicidad se puede originar en una circunstancia concreta; nace, se denuncia, se manifiesta a veces en un punto muy particular, pero envuelve la totalidad de la vida y opera sobre ella una transformación. Cuando una persona es feliz, y en la medida en que lo es, su vida entera queda transfigurada, transformada, las cosas adquieren un sentido nuevo, que no tiene el que no posee ya o no ha llegado a la felicidad. En forma privativa, la infelicidad transforma igualmente la totalidad de la vida, la pone a otra luz, establece una diferente jerarquía entre las cosas: las que parecían importantes dejan de serlo, otras se adelantan hasta el primer plano. El equilibrio global se altera, la configuración de la vida se transforma, los efectos no se limitan al punto originario. [...] Si una persona es feliz en cierta dimensión o actividad, ese vector originariamente feliz aparece dentro del haz de los demás, se derrama sobre ellos y los pone a una nueva luz, con una tonalidad distinta. Por eso, las ocupaciones triviales, en sí mismas ajenas a la felicidad, se transforman cuando se es feliz. [...] [H]acemos mil cosas triviales y que no tienen que ver con la felicidad, pero si somos felices, esas ocupaciones quedan transfiguradas y adquieren una especie de aureola".

Marías argues that the *full* realisation of one's vocation is not just contingently but *intrinsically* impossible—and so human happiness, in its fulfilment, is also *intrinsically* impossible. This is so because living intrinsically involves choosing. Again, *my life* is not a thing but a task, and that task is what we name living—my dealing with the circumstance, my doing with things in the attempt to realise my own vocation. There is, however, no predetermined way to act, but rather I should *decide* each time how to act—that is, I should *imagine* the different possible ways to deal with my circumstance and among them *choose* to carry out the one I feel is the most appropriate. When the way I act aligns with my true intimate vocation, then happiness occurs. Now, Marías notes that choosing consists in preferring one option over other, thereby declining or at least deferring the less preferable option. This means that we are inevitably forced to decline—or at least defer—putting into practice other ways of dealing with the circumstance—that is, other "trajectories". The problem with regard to happiness is that I may be faced with the task of choosing among two (or more) different mutually exclusive trajectories that may both align with my vocation. Each of these two trajectories may align to a greater or lesser degree with my vocation, but both of them nonetheless may be in accordance with it, and so each one may amount to the realisation of my vocation in its own exclusive and so different way—meaning that even if I were to choose the option that best fits with my vocation I would still be declining (or at least deferring) to carry out other trajectories in which my vocation would also and differently be realised. This is why Marías claims that human happiness, in its complete, fulfilled form is "impossible"—throughout life I find myself faced with many situations where I have to choose only one of two or more mutually exclusive trajectories, despite the fact that all of them will, each one in its own different way, amount to the realisation of my vocation.

An example will clarify the point. I am now at this precise moment at home writing this book on Marías's Metaphysical Anthropology. I have decided to write this book because I feel that at this moment in time it is what best aligns with my (philosophical) vocation—which is why right now I am happier immersing myself in the task of writing this book rather than doing any other thing. However, my decision to be writing this book precludes me from writing other books that may, even if right now to a lesser degree, also satisfy my intimate and sincere philosophical vocation. This may not be a momentous loss but just a deference—I may, and I hope I will, write other philosophical books after this one—but the point still stands that my conscious decision to be *right now* writing this book on Marías precludes me from *right now* writing some other book on another philosophical topic wherein my philosophical vocation may also, and in a different way, be realised.

Despite human happiness being impossible in its fulfilled form, according to Marías human happiness is still "necessary" in the sense that all life is happy to some degree and we cannot but seek its fulfilment. This is so because, as already explained, human happiness is not an add-on but the very task of living. In so far as we live, we are seeking the realisation of our (each one his own) vocation—and so we are seeking the realisation of happiness. As Marías puts it: "Aspiration to happiness is unrenounceable, because it coincides with the aspiration which constitutes our life" (Marías 1970a, p. 239 [Marías 1970b, p. 279]). And inasmuch as living consists in projecting myself onto my circumstance with the aim of realising my vocation, the very task of living necessarily implies that, at least to some minimal degree, my vocation becomes realised through my projecting—and so *my life*, and in fact any *human life* in the measure that it engages in the task of living and so of projecting, is necessarily happy even if to an extremely minimal extent.

To sum up, then, and according to Marías, human happiness is impossible in its complete fulfilled form given the character of choice intrinsic to living. Nonetheless, human happiness is still necessary inasmuch as it is identified with the very task of living—explaining, on the one hand, why we cannot stop seeking happiness, and on the other, why all life is happy to some degree even if minimal. Taking these two claims together is what leads Marías to conclude that human happiness is the "necessary impossibility" ("*imposible necesario*"). In *Antropología metafísica*, Marías summarises his argument as follows:

> To the degree that happiness is the realization of aspiration, we would have to say that *all life is happy*, or that one lives in the element of happiness. But to the extent that the aspiration is never sufficiently realized, happiness appears to be impossible. Still more: even supposing that I were always to

choose correctly and that the circumstance always allowed me to carry out my projects, since I cannot carry out more than one of the possible trajectories of my life, and several of these are at every moment desired and desirable, all choice or preference is a delaying or setting-aside of what I would *also* like to be and do. This makes happiness intrinsically impossible for structural reasons. If in one sense it is true that all life is happy, in another perspective we would have to say that *the best of all possible lives is not happy*. This means that life is perpetual, inexorable *dissatisfaction*; but as soon as we have said this we realize that this means that satisfaction is inherent in life, that life moves in the element of satisfaction. (Marías 1970a, p. 240, author's emphasis [Marías 1970b, pp. 280–281])

In *La felicidad humana*, Marías gives a clearer and more extensive formulation of the same reasoning for concluding that human happiness is the "necessary impossibility":

If I have several possibilities before me and I choose one, that one I have chosen does not fully satisfy me, it pains me to have renounced others that I also desired, that equally attracted and called me. Human life consists of a mechanism of choice, of *preference* (to put something in front: *praeferre*, to put in front) and *postponement*. [...] The young person, in principle, can be everything, because he is still almost nothing, and in the measure that he goes on being, that he goes on determining himself, he goes on denying possibilities, he goes on shaping himself with renunciations and exclusions. This is the inexorable condition of human life, and it leads us to a concept I have used very thoroughly [...] because without it human life is not comprehensible. It is, of course, the concept of *trajectories*, and I say it in plural because its true meaning lies precisely in its plurality. We speak, indeed, of the trajectory of a life; but if I simply say what I have done and what has happened to me, I do not present my complete reality, which also includes what I have not done, what could have happened to me but did not happen to me, what I could have done and what I could not, what I have wanted to do and later I have given up, or has been frustrated or has vanished. That is, there is a plurality of trajectories, realised, initiated, abandoned, frustrated, perhaps recovered, and all of that composes my life. [...] This is the fundamental reason why happiness is impossible in this world, even supposing that I always get it right, and moreover supposing that I can realise that which I have chosen and preferred: I must renounce many other things, other trajectories that also attract me, that are *mine*, that ought be realised, and therefore I am not fully happy, even if I have managed to get it right and realise *the best*, because what is not the best also seems *good* to me, and I miss it, its absence pains me. We see how happiness, because of formal conditions, because of the structural conditions of human life, is ultimately not possible, but I cannot renounce to it. (Marías 1987, pp. 29–30, author's emphasis)[10]

According to Marías, our inalienable seeking of happiness inexorably leads us to the certainty of the *necessity* of our (each one his own) death. Living consists in projecting myself onto the world with the aim of realising my vocation. Projecting refers to the future—which as already noted in Chap. 3 is the reason why Marías claims that living is necessarily, as an a priori requirement that is part of the *analytical structure of human life*, future-oriented. By engaging in the very task of living—that is, by projecting myself onto the world in reference to the future—I inexorably reach the certainty that I am necessarily going to die. Death appears to me not just as a possibility but as a necessity, meaning that it is not just that I *can* die but that I *must* die—in Marías's expression, I am not just *mortalis* but *moriturus*. The concrete moment my death will occur is

---

[10] My translation. The original Spanish text reads: "Si tengo ante mí varias posibilidades y elijo una, esa que he elegido no me satisface plenamente, me duele haber renunciado a otras que también deseaba, que igualmente me atraían y me llamaban. La vida humana consiste en un mecanismo de elección, de *preferencia* (poner una cosa delante: *praeferre*, poner delante) y *postergación*. [...] El joven, en principio, puede ser todo, porque todavía no es casi nada, y a medida que va siendo, que se va determinando, va negando posibilidades, se va haciendo con renuncias y exclusiones. Esta es la condición inexorable de la vida humana, y nos lleva a un concepto que he usado muy a fondo [...] porque sin él la vida humana no es comprensible. Se trata, claro es, del concepto de *trayectorias*, y lo digo en plural porque su verdadero sentido estriba precisamente en su pluralidad. Hablamos, ciertamente, de la trayectoria de una vida; pero si digo simplemente lo que he hecho y me ha pasado, no presento mi realidad completa, que incluye además lo que no he hecho, lo que me pudo pasar pero no me pasó, lo que he podido hacer y lo que no pude, lo que he querido hacer y luego he abandonado, o se ha frustrado o desvanecido. Es decir, hay una pluralidad de trayectorias, realizadas, iniciadas, abandonadas, frustradas, tal vez recuperadas, y todo eso compone mi vida. [...] Esta es la razón fundamental de que la felicidad sea imposible en este mundo, aun suponiendo que siempre acierte, y que además pueda realizar eso que he elegido y preferido: tengo que renunciar a otras muchas cosas, a otras trayectorias que también me atraen, que son *mías*, que deberían ser realizadas, y por consiguiente no soy plenamente feliz, aunque haya conseguido acertar y realizar *lo mejor*, porque lo que no es lo mejor también me parece *bueno*, y lo echo de menos, y me duele su ausencia. Vemos cómo la felicidad, por condiciones formales, por las condiciones estructurales de la vida humana, a última hora no es posible, pero no puedo renunciar a ella".

unknown to me, but the *fact* that I am necessarily going to die appears as a certainty to me—a claim which is clearly captured in the Latin formula "*mors certa, hora incerta*":

> Mortality does not mean only that one "can" die, but, moreover, that one "must" die. The combination of both these points of view—one can die at any moment, one must die sometime—is the real mortality of man, unsurpassably expressed in the formula *mors certa, hora incerta*. (Marías 1970a, p. 251, author's emphasis [Marías 1970b, p. 292])

It is important to emphasise that Marías is not *only* making the epistemological claim that I am (each one is) certain that I am going to die. Rather, Marías is arguing that besides being certain to me, the fact that I am going to die is *necessary*. As just explained, I discover the necessity of my death in my own living, through projecting myself onto the world in reference to the future. This necessity is not, however, referred to in the *analytical structure of human life*. The fact that I am going to die, while being necessary, is not found through the metaphysical analysis of *my life*, meaning that it is not an a priori necessary condition for *human life*. The necessity of (my) death is not inferred from the analytical claim that "I am myself and my circumstance" ("*Yo soy yo y mi circumstancia*")—which shows that there is nothing incoherent in the possibility of a *human life* that does not die. Actually, and as will be explained next, according to Marías it is just the contrary—*my life* (each one's) calls for its own indefinite perdurance.

The necessity of (my) death is not an analytical claim, meaning that it should therefore be an empirical one. However, this necessity is not inferred from the observational fact that everyone I have direct or indirect knowledge of has in the end died. This kind of inductive reasoning shows that (my) death is extremely probable, but it does not prove it to be necessary. Of course, no one denies, including Marías, that the probability is so high that this alone suffices to make it epistemically imprudent to hold the belief that I am not going to die, but still this overwhelming probability strictly speaking does not prove its necessity—inasmuch as it does not make inconsistent the possibility of there being an exception.

According to Marías, the necessity of (my) death is grounded in the contingent but still constitutive determinations that shape the concrete realisation of *my life*, and which are nonetheless independent of the concrete contents of my (and anyone's) biography—that is, in the *empirical structure of human life* as I empirically find it realised in myself as the reality *man* that I am. I am necessarily going to die inasmuch as *what* I am is a *man*, and *man* is constitutively *moriturus*. More concretely, the necessity of death is grounded in the empirically contingent but nonetheless constitutive determination of *man* that any *human life* realised in the reality *man* is *installed* in the process of growing old and the succession of ages—starting from childhood, going through puberty, youth and adult age, and ending in old age, which is defined by it being the last age. The process of aging, and the consequent succession of ages or stages of life, while not being an a priori requirement for *human life*, is an intrinsic determination of the reality *man*—and it is intrinsic to old age the fact that it ends in death: "The important thing about old age [...] [is that] 'one can't go beyond old age', which means, if we look at things from inside life, that it is the last age, that there is no further age" (Marías 1970a, p. 217 [Marías 1970b, p. 253]). Therefore, the necessity of (my) death is neither an analytical, metaphysical claim nor a probabilistic, inductively grounded claim, but an *anthropological* claim, grounded in the constitutive determinations of the reality that shapes *what* I am and that we call *man*. Despite having discovered the necessity of my own death through my own living, given that this necessity is an *anthropological* claim and so grounded in the constitutive determinations that shape the reality *man*, I infer that death is a necessary event in any *human life* that is realised in the reality *man*. In Marías's words:

It is not *my life* which inexorably debouches in death; it is *the man I am*. [...] This life has a structure which we call "man"; this structure is "closed"; it has a biological cycle which ends, which does not go on happening indefinitely, which concludes with a last age that we call old age. The life of *man*, biographical life in its real empirical structure, must end. When I take possession of what I am as I really am, I discover myself as mortal and, moreover, as *moriturus*. Hence my certainty of death, and the innumerable "exceptions" of the living avail me not at all. In my own biography, when I project myself as the man I am, I encounter my intrinsic mortality. It is what shapes the trajectory of my life. I project myself in my successive ages, installing myself provisionally in each of them, and then I reach one which is the *last* but which is not definitive: old age. When we say, "one can't go beyond old age", we are encountering the inherent mortality of man; we can neither get past being old nor continue to be old indefinitely. This structure is both limited and closed: that is why it ends in the black hole of death. (Marías 1970a, pp. 254 *and* 256–257, author's emphasis [Marías 1970b, pp. 295 *and* 298])

According to Marías, my certainty of the necessity of my (and each *man's*) death annuls my pursuit of happiness. The problem now is not just that human happiness is intrinsically impossible in its fulfilled form, but that my certainty of the necessity of my (and each *man's*) death impedes me from pursuing happiness. Marías's argument in this regard can be stated as follows. If at some point I am going to die, my living will lose all its significance. There is no reason, no ultimate "for what?" in seeking the realisation of the *who* I am called to be—that is, the realisation of my (each one his own) vocation—if the *who* I am will at some point irremediably fade away—if death altogether annihilates the *who* I am, all my efforts in sticking to the call of my vocation and so in becoming that precise and not another *who* will have been in vain. In the face of death, the pursuit of happiness becomes a futile task—and once we become aware of its futility, the very pursuit of happiness appears to us as a task that is not worth performing, thereby annulling any intention on our part to attempt to achieve it. Accordingly, this means that the pursuit of happiness is only possible on the assumption that the *who* I am will not fade away—and so I will be able to indefinitely futureward project. In other words, and to put it more succinctly, human happiness calls for personal immortality inasmuch as without its assumption engaging in the task of pursuing happiness becomes impracticable. The problem is that I cannot but take death into account—as already explained, I inexorably reach undeniable certainty on the necessity of my (and each *man's*) death in my own living. This means that I do not have to wait until my death occurs to notice that my pursuit of happiness is nothing more than a vain task, thereby already appearing to me right now as an impracticable task. This is why Marías claims that in the face of the necessity of my (and each *man's*) death, and my unavoidable certainty about it, human happiness appears as nothing more than "a cheat" ("*un engaño*"). Happiness seems only possible if I am able to deceive myself with the attempt to forget about the undeniable certainty of the necessity of my (and each *man's*) death—but this attempt is simply unfeasible because, as already explained, the necessary future-oriented character of living inexorably leads me right now to the certainty of the *anthropological* necessity of my (and each *man's*) death:

> If I die altogether, at some point everything will cease to matter to me; therefore it is a question of waiting. Nothing really matters, therefore nothing *is worth doing*. And if this is true, no one can be happy except in the measure that he can provisionally forget death. Happiness would be, in the end, a cheat. We must get used to calling things by their name. Now, death is an ingredient of human life; life appears to us affected by mortality, threatened by it at every instant, called to it. Death makes happiness impossible, illusory, deceptive; but happiness is necessary, for it is the very reality of life. Death means, therefore, the inner emptiness of life, its annulment. (Marías 1970a, p. 248, author's emphasis [Marías 1970b, p. 289])

As Marías puts it in the last two sentences of the previous quote, my awareness of the necessity of my (and each *man's*) death does not only impede the pursuit of happiness but the very task of living too. Since according to Marías human happiness is not an add-on but the result of the realisation of living, the claim that my inexorable awareness of the necessity of my (and each *man's*) death impedes my pursuit of happiness is tantamount to claiming that it impedes me from carrying out the very task of living. Therefore, as with the pursuit of happiness, living turns out to be impracticable unless under the assumption of its own indefinite perdurance—that is, under the assumption that the task of living will go on indefinitely.

Now, and this is a crucial step, since *my life* is not a thing but a task, and this task is living, Marías's claim that living is impracticable unless on the assumption of its own indefinite perdurance shows this assumption to be an a priori necessary requirement without which *my life* (each one's) is *impossible*—and since *my life* (each one's) is the *radical reality* in which all other realities are *radicated*, this is tantamount to claiming that such an assumption is an ontological requirement without which all reality is *impossible.*

Once the conceptual leap between human happiness and living has been made, Marías's argument is no longer just that personal immortality is a convenient presupposition that I myself should make to make of living a task more worth engaging in. His contention now is that the assumption of personal immortality is an actual ontological requirement without which living, and so *my life* as *radical reality*, is *impossible*. This means that, strictly speaking, it is not I myself, the executive I, but *my life* as *radical reality* that necessarily assumes its own indefinite perdurance. Since *my life* is not an intentional agent, assumption here should not be understood as an epistemic attitude. Rather, *my life's* (each one's) assumption in its own indefinite perdurance should be understood as a necessary *postulate*, intrinsic to the reality *my life* and therefore without which *my life* itself is *impossible*—*my life*, and these are the exact words Marías uses, "[...] *postula su permanencia, su indefinida e ilimitada permanencia*" ("[...] postulates its permanence, its indefinite and unlimited persistence") (Marías 1970a, p. 264 [Marías 1970b, p. 305]). It is important to emphasise that what is intrinsic to *my life* (each one's) is the *assumption* of its own indefinite perdurance—there is no a priori analytical reason implying that *my life* will necessarily perdure indefinitely, meaning that the annihilation of *my life* (each one's) is still a conceptual possibility. In other words, *my life* (each one's) is only possible in the measure that its own indefinite perdurance is taken for granted—but this does not imply that, as a matter of fact, *my life* will perdure indefinitely.

Therefore, and according to Marías, the assumption of its own indefinite perduration is an intrinsic determination of *my life*. This indefinite perdurance refers to *my life* in its entirety, so now it is not just about the *who* I am but also about the circumstance that I happen to coexist with. It is worth pointing out two implications that follow from this claim. First, since the assumption of the indefinite perdurance of *my life* is not an *anthropological* requirement but (apparently) an analytical requirement of *my life*, it therefore applies to any *human life* regardless of its concrete realisation on this or that concrete *empirical structure*. This means that not just *man* but any other conceivable form of *human life*, in so far as they *live*, and they necessarily do so because this is what the reality of any *human life* consists of, is already presupposing their own indefinite perdurance. Second, and on which Marías's connection between his Metaphysical Anthropology and the call for Christian Salvation through Resurrection relies, which will be commented in detail in Chap. 5 of this book, this indefinite perdurance refers to *my life* in its entirety and as such it is fully personal. Therefore, it does not just involve the *who* I am but also my circumstance, the world I happen to coexist with. And among my circumstance it is included, as constitutive elements of it: *first*, that concrete and precise personal reality whom I found *radicated* in *my life* as being part of my circumstance and with whom I am in love; and *second*, the kind of worldly corporeal installation in which *my life* already happens to be realised and which gives to *my life* its empirical concreteness as that concrete *man* that I am and not other.

To sum up, therefore, and according to Marías, *my life* (each one's) presupposes, not as an epistemic attitude but as an intrinsic postulate without which *my life* itself is *impossible*, the assumption of its own indefinite perdurance. This is the crucial claim in Marías's argumentation. Ultimately, this is what serves Marías to transform the problem of the futility of life in face of the *anthropological* necessity of death—which is by itself a *practical problem* as Marías rightly frames it when first formulating it in relation to human happiness—into an *ontological problem* regarding the very reality *man*. The ultimate problem is now not that the necessity of my (and each *man*'s) death makes of living a futile task— admittedly, this is still a serious problem—but that the *anthropological* necessity of death contradicts one of the necessary requirements of the *radical reality* that is *my life*, thereby making it *impossible*.

The reality *man* appears therefore to be positioned in a seemingly unsolvable contradictory situation, involving two undeniable and apparently irreconcilable claims. While *my life* is only possible on the assumption of its own indefinite perdurance, I cannot deny that, inasmuch as being a *man*, I am *necessarily* going to die. Putting it more formally, and using Marías's terminology, the contradiction seems to rely on the very realisation of *human life* in the reality *man*: the necessity of death is part of the *empirical structure of human life* as we find it realised in *man*— meaning that death is an empirically contingent but nonetheless constitutive determination of the reality *man*—while the assumption of the indefinite perduration of *my life* is part of the *analytical structure of human life*—meaning that it is an intrinsic determination of *my life* (and so a priori necessary to any *human life* regardless of its concrete *empirical structure*). Marías condensed this argument in the following quote from *Antropología metafísica*:

> The empirical structure of human life—what we call "man"— is "closed", and leads to his mortality. The projective and future-oriented structure of biographical life as such is "open" and plotlike, and in this sense postulates its permanence, its indefinite and unlimited persistence. If "man" is intrinsically mortal, "my life" consists in an aspiration to eternity. (Marías 1970a, p. 264 [Marías 1970b, p. 305])

The contradiction becomes apparent, Marías argues, when we spell out what death means. There are two different meanings involved in the term death that are often confused but should be clearly distinguished: *biological death* and *personal death*. *Biological death* refers to the loss of my (each one his own) corporeal installation, and it may occur to all living organisms in that they are corporeally installed. *Personal death* refers to the annihilation of *my life* as *radical reality*, and as such it can only occur to personal or biographical beings—that is, it can only occur to a *human life*, regardless of its concrete *empirical structure*.

The distinction between *biological death* and *personal death* allows Marías to dissolve the apparent contradiction lying in the realisation of *human life* as *man*. According to Marías, what I find in my own living is the necessity of my (and each *man*'s) *biological death*—that is, the *anthropologically* necessary fact that, as long as no external causes are involved and so no fatal accident happens to me, I will go on aging until after spending an indeterminate length of time being elderly, I will end up losing my concrete corporeal installation. However, I have no evidence to conclude the necessity of my *personal death*—actually, and as just explained, according to Marías it is precisely the contrary: *my life* calls for its own indefinite perdurance. Moreover, strictly speaking my *personal death* is unintelligible to me. As already explained, *my life* is the *radical reality*, meaning that everything I can relate to it, be it theoretically or practically, is *radicated* in *my life*. Apprehension of *my personal death* is unintelligible to me since I cannot imagine the annihilation of *my life* unless as a *radicated reality*—that is, rooted in *my life* as part of my circumstance—but in doing so I would already be presupposing the reality of *my life* and so denying its annihilation. Neither does my experience of the death of others shed any light on my understanding of *personal death* since my experience is restricted to their *biological death* inasmuch as I do not have *immediate* apprehension of their *lives* as *radical reality*.

Of course, it may be argued, and Marías obviously acknowledges this possibility, that *biological death* causes *personal death*. However, Marías points out that this would just be a theory or an interpretation of death, in the sense that it is a further interpretative step that does not eliminate the conceptual distinction between *biological death* and *personal death,* but rather argues for a causal relation between them. Furthermore, it is an extremely problematic interpretation inasmuch as first, *personal death* is unintelligible to us, and second, because *my life* is not reduced to my corporeal installation—I am not my body, as those who straightforwardly claim that *biological death* causes *personal death* would most probably be presupposing. Regarding this, it is important to note that in distinguishing between *personal death* and *biological death,* Marías is neither presupposing nor advocating for any sort of dualism. My *biological death* consists in the loss of my corporeal installation. I am not a body, but neither is my body a *thing* that I possess and that *biological death* takes away from me. I am neither my body nor, strictly speaking, is my body mine, but rather I am corporeal—that is, I am *installed* in a body, and more precisely in this concrete body, which I call "mine" despite, strictly speaking, it not being a thing that I possess. This is why *biological death*, even while being restricted to the loss of my corporeal installation and so being distinct from *personal death*, is still *my* death—it occurs to me, affecting my concrete corporeal installation as the concrete *man* that I am.

Marías's distinction between *biological death* and *personal death* is drawn throughout the last two chapters of *Antropología metafísica*, and is nicely summarised in the following passage of *La felicidad humana*:

> *Man* must die, but *life* is an open structure that postulates immortality. [...] [B]iological death [is] something that happens at every moment (also with animals and even with plants, with differences that come from the various

forms of life), a perfectly explicable process, the suspension of vital func-
tions, the destruction of an organism; but if we take *my* death, the death of
someone, of someone personal, we find something completely different. It
will be said that yes, but that it *is caused by* the biological death. This is conceivable, but in any case, it would be *two* deaths: the death of an organism
and the death of a person. Their connection is a theory, of course a problematic one, an open question. *That which* I am is mortal; but *who* I am consist
in aspiring to be immortal. Moreover, man cannot imagine not being,
because if I imagine myself as non-existent, I do so *from life*, as if I were com-
ing back to see what has happened. Personal death cannot be imagined but
from life and its aspiration to immortality. This is rigorously descriptive and
indubitable. (Marías 1987, pp. 322–323, author's emphasis)[11]

The conceptual distinction between *biological death* and *personal
death*, together with Marías's claim that corporeality is an *anthropological*
installation and so is not an a priori necessary requirement for *my life*
but a contingent determination of it that may therefore vary, allows
Marías to dissolve the apparent contradiction regarding the reality *man*.[12]
Once the distinction is made, there seems to be no conceptual reason for
denying the possibility that *my life* may continue after my *biological*

---

[11] My translation. The original Spanish text reads: "El *hombre* tiene que morir, pero la *vida* es una
estructura abierta que postula la inmortalidad. […] la muerte biológica, algo que acontece en cada
momento (también con los animales y hasta con las plantas, con diferencias que proceden de las
diversas formas de vida), un proceso perfectamente explicable, suspensión de funciones vitales,
destrucción de un organismo; pero si tomamos *mi* muerte, la muerte de *alguien*, personal, encontramos algo completamente distinto. Se dirá que sí, pero que se produce *a causa* de la muerte
biológica. Es posible, pero en todo caso serían *dos* muertes: la muerte de un organismo y la muerte
de una persona. Su conexión es una teoría, por supuesto problemática, una cuestión abierta. *Lo que*
yo soy es mortal; pero *quien* soy consiste en pretender ser inmortal. Además, el hombre no puede
imaginarse no siéndolo, porque si me imagino como no existente, lo hago *desde la vida*, como si
volviera para ver lo que ha pasado. No se puede imaginar la muerte personal más que desde la vida
y de su pretensión de inmortalidad. Esto es rigurosamente descriptivo e indudable".

[12] It is important to note, however, and this will be explained in greater detail in Chap. 5 in relation
to Christian Resurrection, that despite corporeality being an *anthropological* installation and *human
life* being conceivable under different types of worldly installations, the kind of indefinite perdurance intrinsically postulated by *my life* (each one's) refers to the same *qualitative* worldly corporeal
installation in which *my life* already happens to be realised, even if it is *numerically* distinct—otherwise such a life would not be the *same* life. This means that even if *my life* may be conceivable in
a completely different worldly installation, even in a disembodied form, the kind of indefinite
perdurance *my life* (each one's) postulates refers to my (each one's) worldly corporeal installation in
which *my life* is already realised.

death—inasmuch as there is no a priori conceptual reason for denying that after the loss of my current corporeal installation, *my life* may be realised (better said, transformed) on another concrete *empirical structure*.

Let me emphasise that Marías's argumentation is not, and neither aims to be, an argument for *proving* an after earthly death existence. Rather, the aim of Marías's argumentation is to show that our *hoping* for personal immortality is justified as it being a self-affirming exercise, our conscious endorsement of what constitutes our *human* reality. The crucial point in Marías's argumentation relies on his already commented reasoning for concluding that not (at least not only) I myself, the executive I, but *my life* in its entirety assumes, as an intrinsic postulate without which *my life* as *radical reality* is *impossible*, its own indefinite perdurance. Marías's distinction between *biological death* and *personal death* is just a conceptual distinction, and as such it is not by itself a philosophical argument. The distinction is, however, philosophically relevant inasmuch as it allows the *anthropological* necessity of *biological death* without thereby making *personal death* necessary—that is, it allows the conceptual possibility that after my *biological death* occurs, *my life* may be transformed onto another *empirical structure* which, albeit necessarily numerically different in its concrete corporeal installation, may still be *my life*.

To put it more succinctly, Marías's argument ultimately arises from his claim that unless on the assumption of its own indefinite perdurance, *my life* as *radical reality* (and so any *human life*) is *impossible*. It should again be emphasised that what is intrinsic to *my life* (each one's) is the *assumption* of its own indefinite perdurance, not the fact that it will perdure indefinitely—so *personal death*, the occasional annihilation of *my life* (each one's), is still a conceptual possibility. Moreover, *my life's* assumption of its own indefinite perdurance is not an *anthropological* requirement but an *analytical* requirement, and so a priori necessary for any *human life* regardless of its concrete realisation—meaning that it applies to any *human life* no matter its *empirical structure*. More importantly, and as mentioned before, it is an intrinsic postulate without which *my life* (each one's) as *radical reality* is *impossible*, but strictly speaking it is not an epistemic attitude of part of I myself, the executive I. However, and here is the crucial point, this assumption being an intrinsic postulate of *my life* (each one's) justifies my conscious endorsement of it by part of I myself, the executive I. Under these premises, although *personal death* remains as an equally open possibility as its indefinite perdurance is, my conscious hope for personal immortality becomes justified inasmuch as it amounts to a self-affirming exercise, a conscious endorsement of my own *human* reality and so also a sign of authenticity. Of course, justification here should not be understood in its epistemic, truth-oriented sense, but in the sense of showing that my conscious hope for personal immortality is a legitimate attitude on my part. This conscious hope of mine will certainly allow my pursuit of happiness, but again it is important not to confuse Marías's argument with a pragmatic reasoning—Marías's contention is that my conscious hope for personal immortality is justified as it being my conscious endorsement of what ultimately consists of my own *human* reality, but not because it is a convenient presupposition that may make the task of living something more bearable.

The crux of Marías's argument is his identification between human happiness and the task of living. It allows Marías to identify the conditions for human happiness as conditions for *my life* (each one's)—and given that *my life* is the *radical reality*, these conditions turn out to be an ontological requirement without which all reality is *impossible*. This identification, however, involves a conceptual leap not made explicit by Marías. By identifying human happiness, which according to Marías himself is an installation, with the task of living, which is what *my life* consists of, Marías is leaping from the *empirical structure of human life* to the *analytical structure of human life*—and so from the while constitutive still contingent determinations regarding the concrete way in which *my life* happens to be realised to its a priori necessary determinations. This conceptual leap is highly problematic even conceding one and each of the premises involved in Marías's Metaphysical Anthropology.

The identification between human happiness and the task of living undermines the very motivation behind the distinction between the *analytical structure of human life* and the *empirical structure of human life*—which, as already explained in Chap. 3, is that of offering a clear-cut distinction between, on the one hand, the a priori necessary intrinsic determinations of *my life* (and so of any *human life*) and, on the other, the constitutive but still empirically contingent determinations that shape the concrete realisation of *my life* (each one's). According to Marías himself, and as already explained in Chap. 3, being installed is an analytical requirement for any *human life*, but the fact of being installed in such and such a concrete way and not in another is an empirically contingent fact regarding the concrete way that a particular *human life* happens to be realised. However, Marías's identification of human happiness with living implies that human happiness, despite being a concrete installation and so apparently not being an a priori necessary determination of *my life*, is nonetheless a necessary installation of any *human life* regardless of its concretisation. Marías does not explicitly make the claim that human happiness is a necessary installation of any *human life*, but he probably must have been aware of it being a consequence of his identification between human happiness and living. In fact, I would say that this is the reason why in all his texts Marías uses the term "*human* happiness" instead of "happiness of *man*", or more simply and naturally just "happiness"—thereby hinting that human happiness, given its identification with the task of living, is a necessary installation pertaining to any *human life* no matter its concrete realisation on this or that *empirical structure*. There may be no contradiction in allowing the possibility of an installation that is necessarily present in any *human life*—and so pertaining to the *analytical structure of human life*. But this claim would require, under the methodological premises of Marías's Metaphysical Anthropology, that such installation is found through the metaphysical analysis of *my life*. There is no argument in this direction in Marías's writings—and it seems that there cannot be one.

The claim that the realisation of the task of living leads to the installation of human happiness is not inferred from the "*Yo soy yo y mi circumstancia*" ("I am myself and my circumstance"). Let us concede to Marías that I (each one of us) find, in my own living and therefore empirically, that my success in projecting myself onto my circumstance with the aim of realising my own vocation or vital programme leads me to a particular installation which I, following Marías, decide to name as "human happiness". Even conceding that this is so, this concrete installation which, following Marías, I name as human happiness is not found through the metaphysical analysis of *my life*—that is, even accepting that *my life* (and so any *human life*) is a priori necessarily projective and directed to the realisation of my (each one his own) vocation or vital programme, this does not imply that the realisation of this vocation will necessarily lead to that concrete installation that we, following Marías, have decided to name as human happiness. The claim that the realisation of my (each one his own) vocation leads me to become installed in human happiness is not therefore an analytical claim but an empirical one. It is exclusively grounded in my own empirical observation regarding the results of my success in the realisation of my vocation, and is clearly not inferred from any a priori necessary requirement of *my life*. So although human happiness may perhaps be a constitutive installation of *man,* this still does not preclude the possibility of there being a *human life* distinct from *man* which, even if still projective and directed towards the realisation of his own vocation, may be realised on a different empirical structure that lacks the installation of human happiness. This means that, contrary to Marías's contention, human happiness cannot be identified with living—and so even conceding that the pursuit of human happiness requires the assumption of the indefinite perdurance of living, this does not imply that the assumption of its own indefinite perdurance is a necessary determination without which *my life* (each one's) as *radical reality* is itself *impossible*.

If this is so, Marías's claim that the realisation of our (each one his own) vocation leads to the concrete installation of human happiness becomes, at best, an *anthropological* claim and as such restricted to the reality *man*. This clearly undermines Marías's identification of human happiness with living, and so his claim that the conditions for human happiness are conditions for *my life* (each one's). Certainly, on this basis it might still be argued that the assumption of his own indefinite perdurance is a condition for *man* to pursue his happiness, but now there is no reason to claim that *my life* (each one's) as *radical reality* presupposes, as an intrinsic ontological postulate without which it itself is *impossible*, its own indefinite perdurance. Accordingly, it might still be argued that *man* needs to hope for his own personal immortality so as to enjoy of a happy life, and that this need by itself may justify consciously endorsing such hope, but this would be a pragmatic argument aiming to show that hoping for personal immortality is a convenient presupposition—or even a practically necessary presupposition if we are to concede that for *man* the very task of living becomes impracticable without hope for his own personal immortality. Of course, this line of reasoning would still be interesting. However, my point is that this is not what Marías contended. Rather, his contention is to convert the *practical need* of presupposing one's own indefinite perdurance to face the futility of living in the face of our inexorable certainty about the *anthropological* necessity of *biological death* into an *ontological postulate* referring to the indefinite perdurance of *my life* (each one's) and without which *my life* as *radical reality* is itself *impossible* (and so all reality inasmuch as, under Marías's premises, any reality must be *radicated* in *my life*)—thereby showing that consciously hoping for personal immortality is justified not because of its practical convenience but because it is a self-affirming exercise, a conscious endorsement of our own *human* reality and so a sign of authenticity.

References

Marías, J. (1952a) 1971. Human Happiness: The World and Paradise. In *Philosophy as Dramatic Theory*, trans. James Parsons, 201–227. Pennsylvania: The Pennsylvania State University Press.

Marías, J. (1952b) 1959. La felicidad humana: mundo y paraíso. In *Julián Marías: Obras (vol. IV)*, 364–382. Madrid: Revista de Occidente.

Marías, J. (1970a) 1971. *Metaphysical Anthropology: The Empirical Structure of Human Life*. Trans. Frances M. López-Morillas. Pennsylvania: The Pennsylvania State University Press.

Marías, J. (1970b). *Antropología metafísica: la estructura empírica de la vida humana*. Madrid: Revista de Occidente.

Marías, J. (1987). *La felicidad humana*. Madrid: Alianza Editorial.

Marías, J. (1995). *Tratado de lo mejor: la moral y las formas de vida*. Madrid: Alianza Editorial.

5

Julián Marías on Resurrection and the Call for Christian Salvation

Abstract This chapter analyses Marías's argumentation for concluding that my (each one's) conscious hope for Christian Salvation through Resurrection is justified as it being a conscious endorsement of my own *human* reality. The different steps involved in Marías's argumentation are examined. It is shown that Marías's argumentation in this regard ultimately relies on the claim that only if the Christian God were to exist and save us through Resurrection would the ontological postulate intrinsic to *my life* (each one's) regarding its own indefinite perdurance then be satisfied. It is also shown that Marías's argumentation involves an argumentative transition from the premises of his Metaphysical Anthropology to the religious interpretation of Christian Revelation. It is argued that such an argumentative step is unproblematic, from both a philosophical and a Christian point of view.

Keywords Christianity • Christian Resurrection • Hope • Immortality • Jesus Christ • Julián Marías • Love • Revelation

© The Author(s), under exclusive license to Springer Nature Switzerland AG 2024
A. Oya, *The Metaphysical Anthropology of Julián Marías*, Palgrave Frontiers in Philosophy of Religion, https://doi.org/10.1007/978-3-031-61804-8_5

According to Marías, and as discussed in Chap. 4, *my life* (each one's) presupposes, not as an epistemic attitude on the part of I myself, the executive I, but as an *intrinsic ontological postulate* without which *my life* itself as *radical reality* is *impossible*, the assumption of its own indefinite perdurance. *My life* (each one's) is therefore only possible provided that it takes for granted its own indefinite perdurance—and since *my life* (each one's) is the *radical reality* in which all other realities are *radicated*, this is tantamount to claiming that *my life*'s postulate of its own indefinite perdurance is an ontological requirement without which all reality is *impossible*. This ontological postulate is intrinsic to *my life*, which is what allows Marías to justify my (each one's) conscious *hope* for the indefinite perdurance of *my life* after my *biological death* occurs as this being a self-affirming exercise, a conscious endorsement of my own *human* reality, and so a sign of authenticity. This ontological postulate does not, however, allow us to prove the indefinite perdurance of *my life* (each one's), inasmuch as it does not imply that, as a matter of fact, *my life* will perdure indefinitely—*personal death*, the occasional annihilation of *my life* as *radical reality*, is still a conceptual possibility. Therefore, since *personal death* remains an equally open possibility as the indefinite perdurance of *my life*, justification here should not be understood in its truth-oriented sense, as aiming to show that my (each one's) conscious *hope* for the indefinite perdurance of *my life* is justified on the grounds that this indefinite perdurance will in fact occur, but rather in the sense of showing that that conscious hope of mine is justified as it being a legitimate reaction on my part, inasmuch as it does not contravene my own ultimate *human* reality but actually constitutes a conscious endorsement of it.

The kind of indefinite perdurance that *my life* (each one's) intrinsically postulates is fully personal in the sense of it referring to *my life* as *radical reality* in its entirety. Therefore, and this will be explained next in greater detail, what is postulated is not only the indefinite perdurance of the *who* I am, the executive I, but also the indefinite perdurance of my circumstance. According to Marías, among my circumstance is included, not extrinsically but as a *constitutive* determination of my circumstance without which *my life* as *radical reality* would cease to be the *same* concrete reality: first, that concrete and precise personal reality whom I found *radicated* in *my life* as being part of my circumstance and with whom I am in love; and second, the kind of worldly corporeal installation in which *my life* already happens to be realised and which gives *my life* its empirical concreteness as the concrete *man* that I am and not another.

As Marías rightly points out, the only kind of indefinite perdurance after *biological death* we are aware of that claims the indefinite perdurance of both, of the executive I and of my circumstance, is Christian Salvation through Resurrection, as announced and said to be exemplified by Jesus Christ—which amounts to claiming that only if the Christian God were to exist and save us through Resurrection would the ontological postulate intrinsic to *my life* regarding its indefinite perdurance be satisfied. This is, in brief, what allows Marías to conclude that my (each one's) conscious hope for Christian Salvation through Resurrection is justified as it being a conscious endorsement of my own *human* reality. It should be noted once again that justification here is not to be understood in its truth-oriented sense—Marías's argumentation is not, and does not aim to be, an argument for proving the *truth* (nor even the likelihood) of the factual claim that God actually exists, or for proving that Salvation through Resurrection will, as a matter of fact, actually occur. Again, justification here should be understood in terms of it showing that my (each one's) conscious hope for Christian Salvation through Resurrection is a reaction of mine that is not just consistent with but a conscious endorsement of my own ultimate *human* reality—inasmuch as only if this Salvation were to occur would that ontological postulate intrinsic to *my life* (each one's) be satisfied.

Marías's argumentation is, of course, much richer and more complex than simply consisting in pointing out that the kind of after earthly death existence claimed by Christianity preserves my (each one's) full personal reality. However, the truth remains that it ultimately relies on the claim that only if the Christian God were to exist and save us through Resurrection would the ontological postulate intrinsic to *my life* (each one's) referring to its own indefinite perdurance then be satisfied. This is the crucial premise that allows Marías to step from my (each one's) conscious hope for the indefinite perdurance of *my life* (each one's) to my conscious hope for Christian Salvation through Resurrection.

The aim of this chapter is to discuss Marías's argumentation for concluding that my (each one's) conscious hope for Christian Salvation through Resurrection is justified as it being a conscious endorsement of my own *human* reality and so a self-affirming exercise and a sign of authenticity. Before proceeding further, it is crucial to note that Marías's argumentation in this regard involves an argumentative step from philosophical reasoning to the religious interpretation of Christian Revelation. That is, Marías's argumentation involves an argumentative transition from the premises involved in his Metaphysical Anthropology, which as already explained in the previous chapters of this book are stated in philosophical terms and exclusively formulated through philosophical reasoning, to the interpretation of the contents of Christian Revelation, which is made at a *religious level*—that is, within religion, on its assumption and with no pretension of proving its truth, but with the exclusive aim of understanding its meaning. The step from philosophical reasoning to religious interpretation is unproblematic from a philosophical point of view inasmuch as Marías is consciously careful not to confuse the two argumentative levels—that is, he is careful not to attempt to justify the premises of his Metaphysical Anthropology on the basis of Christian Revelation, nor to attempt to justify the contents of Christian Revelation on the basis of his Metaphysical Anthropology. From a Christian point of view, neither is Marías's ability to conjoin these two argumentative levels, and to do so without confusing them, problematic. In fact, I think this should be considered one of his main merits, inasmuch as he succeeds in formulating a coherent defence of hope for Christian Salvation which, as we will see next, preserves the foundational role of the Biblical testimony about the Resurrection of Jesus Christ and its revealed, non-demonstrable character. However, and while such an argumentative step is not in itself problematic, to clearly comprehend Marías's argumentation it is crucial to make a clear distinction between the claims that are inferred from his Metaphysical Anthropology and those that are inferred from his analysis of Christian Revelation. Otherwise, Marías's contention may be easily misread to be justifying the contents of Christian Revelation on the grounds of his Metaphysical Anthropology—which, as we will see next, is far from being his intention.

Marías was, of course, well aware of his own argumentative step from philosophical reasoning to the religious interpretation of Christian

Revelation. In this regard, it is interesting to note that in his *Antropología metafísica: la estructura empírica de la vida human* (Marías 1970b) [*Metaphysical Anthropology: The Empirical Structure of Human Life* (Marías 1970a)] (hereafter referred to as *Antropología metafísica*), which as already explained in Chap. 2 Marías himself considered as his major philosophical work, he is careful to keep within the exclusively philosophical argumentative level—therefore, although in the book he makes a few religion-related claims, there is no explicit mention of the claim that only if Christian Salvation through Resurrection were to occur would the ontological postulate intrinsic to *my life* (each one's) regarding its own indefinite perdurance be satisfied. On the contrary, in his *La felicidad humana* (Marías 1987) [*The Human Happiness*], although Marías is still careful not to confuse the two argumentative levels, his philosophical reasoning relating to the premises of his Metaphysical Anthropology appears conjoined with his own religious interpretation of the contents of Christian Revelation. Marías's most systematic and exhaustive account of his religious interpretation of Christian Revelation is found in *La perspectiva cristiana* (Marías 1999b) [*The Christian Perspective* (Marías 1999a)].

Marías's argumentation begins on an exclusively philosophical level, with no reference to religion. Its starting point is his claim that my (each one's) conscious hope for personal immortality after my *biological death* occurs is justified as it being a conscious endorsement of my own *human* reality. As already explained in Chap. 4, Marías's argumentation for this claim is exclusively philosophical, with no reference to religion. Ultimately, it is grounded in his identification of human happiness with living— which allows Marías to claim that *my life* (each one's) presupposes, as an *intrinsic ontological postulate* without which *my life* itself as *radical reality* is *impossible*, the assumption of its own indefinite perdurance. Neither is Marías's already commented conceptual distinction between *biological death* and *personal death*, the relevance of which relies on preserving the anthropological necessity of *biological death* without thereby necessarily implying the complete annihilation of *my life* as *radical reality*, inferred from any religious statement, but from the central premises of his Metaphysical Anthropology—more concretely, and as explained in detail in Chap. 4, the distinction is inferred from Marías's claims that: first, *personal death* is unintelligible to us (which, in its turn, is inferred from conceiving *my life* as *radical reality*); and second, that corporeality is an anthropological installation pertaining to the *empirical structure of human life*, and so a contingent determination of *human life*, which may therefore, in principle, vary without this variation implying the annihilation of *my life*.

The kind of indefinite perdurance that *my life* (each one's) intrinsically postulates refers to *my life* itself as *radical reality*—that is, it refers to *my life* in its entirety. As already explained in Chap. 3, *my life* not only involves the I myself, the *who* I am, but also includes my circumstance, the world I happen to coexist with and with which I have to deal—"*Yo soy yo y mi circumstancia, y si no la salvo a ella no me salvo yo*" ("I am myself and my circumstance, and if I do not save it I do not save myself"), in Ortega's formula. Therefore, in addition to referring to the *who* I am, the kind of indefinite perdurance that *my life* intrinsically postulates also refers to the indefinite perdurance of the world I happen to coexist with, my circumstance (each one's). It should be noted once more that this claim is exclusively inferred from Marías's Metaphysical Anthropology, so we are still on the philosophical level of Marías argumentation—more concretely, and as just explained, the claim that the kind of indefinite perdurance that *my life* intrinsically postulates involves both, the I myself and my circumstance, is inferred from Marías's (and Ortega's) claim that *my life* (each one's) as *radical reality* involves the coexistence between I myself and my circumstance, together with Marías's claim that the kind of indefinite perdurance that *my life* intrinsically postulates refers to *my life* itself in its entirety.

Marías's most explicit formulation of his claim that the kind of indefinite perdurance that *my life* intrinsically postulates also involves my circumstance is found in his *Tratado de lo mejor: la moral y las formas de vida* (Marías 1995) [*Treatise on the Best: The Moral and the Ways of Life*]. In this book, and echoing Miguel de Unamuno's affirmation that the kind of immortality we all seek for is that of endlessly continuing to be the same "man of flesh and bone" ("*hombre de carne y hueso*") that we are here and now in this our earthly living, Marías states that the kind of indefinite perdurance *my life* (each one's) intrinsically postulates refers to the "man of flesh and bone and world" ("*hombre de carne y hueso y mundo*").[1] With this formula, Marías is making the claim that what gives *my life* (each one's) its concreteness, what makes it be this concrete life and not another, is not only the *who* I am but also my circumstance, the world I happen to coexist with and with which I have to deal—and, as will be explained next, among my circumstance is also included the same kind of worldly corporeal installation in which *my life* already happens to be realised as the concrete *man* that I am and not another. In Marías's words:

> It is often said, when one wants to express, against all abstract vision, the concreteness of human life, "the *man of flesh and bone*". This is an acceptable formula, but simplified and, therefore, incomplete: it reflects an echo of the interpretation of man as an organism that is always ready to resprout. I think "*and world*" should be added. [...] If one wants to understand man, one must see him in his *world* with all its ingredients, which intervene in the meaning and justification of his actions, and therefore in his morality. But there is something more: this world is not only a "where" in which man is, but a constituent of him, part of his reality. The true effective and living [reality] *includes it*—it is distinct, but inseparable from the I, as is the body. Both realities, body and world, should be understood from the higher unity of the person to whom they belong: *my* world and *my* body, without which I am not *I*. (Marías 1995, p. 45, author's emphasis)[2]

The claim that the kind of indefinite perdurance that *my life* (each one's) intrinsically postulates also involves the indefinite perdurance of my circumstance adds an important condition for the fulfilment of this ontological postulate. In principle, and under the premises of Marías's

---

[1] Marías's and Unamuno's positions on philosophy of religion will be contrasted in Chap. 6 of this book.

[2] My translation. The original Spanish text reads: "Se suele decir, cuando se quiere expresar, frente a toda visión abstracta, la concreción de la vida humana: el *hombre de carne y hueso*. Es una fórmula aceptable, pero simplificada y por tanto incompleta: refleja un eco de la interpretación del hombre como un organismo, que está siempre dispuesta a rebrotar. Creo que hay que añadir: *y mundo*. [...] Si se quiere entender al hombre, hay que verlo en su *mundo* con todos sus ingredientes, que intervienen en el sentido y en la justificación de sus actos, y por tanto en su moralidad. Pero hay algo más: ese mundo no es sólo un 'dónde' en que el hombre se encuentra, sino un constitutivo suyo, parte de su realidad. La verdadera, efectiva y viviente, *lo incluye*, es distinto, pero inseparable del yo, como lo es el cuerpo. Ambas realidades, cuerpo y mundo, han de entenderse desde la unidad superior de la persona de quien son: *mi* mundo y *mi* cuerpo, sin los cuales no soy *yo*".

Metaphysical Anthropology, there seems to be no conceptual reason for denying the possibility that after my *biological death* occurs *my life* will involve a completely different circumstance—after all, my current concrete circumstance is a contingent determination of *my life*, dependent on the concrete way in which *my life* contingently happens to occur. Marías agrees that part of my circumstance is extrinsic to *my life*, and that these extrinsic circumstantial elements may therefore vary without this variation affecting the concreteness of *my life* (each one's). However, and according to Marías, there are elements of my circumstance which are constitutive of *my life* inasmuch as without them *my life* as *radical reality* would lose its concreteness—that is, without them *my life* would no longer be the *same* life. A drastic variation in these constitutive elements of my circumstance will therefore transform *my life* into another completely different *life*, which will then no longer be the *same* concrete reality it is now. So, strictly speaking, a drastic variation in the constitutive elements of my circumstance, even although this variation is still a conceptual possibility as long as the a priori requirements pertaining to the *analytical structure of human life* are met, would amount to my *personal death*—that is, to the annihilation of *my life* as the *concrete* reality it is now. In *La felicidad humana*, Marías makes this point when claiming that the kind of existence after *biological death*, if such an existence were to occur and if it were to meet the ontological postulate referring to the indefinite perdurance of *my life* (each one's), should be interpreted as another act "of the *same* drama that is my life":

> [...] the other life [...] should be interpreted as *another act of the drama*; it is understood, of the *same* drama that is my life. The circumstantiality of human life certainly imposes, after death, a loss of the worldly circumstance, a step to another—it is what has always been named as "the other world"; but this loss must be *partial*. In this life, I always carry with me part of my circumstance, even if it constantly changes as a whole. Certainly, this cannot be applied literally if it is about the other life, the other world, but if *I am I and my circumstance* ["*yo soy yo y mi circumstancia*"] (I do not just "have" circumstance, nor am I just circumstantial), there are ingredients of it that essentially constitute my life, that are ingredients of my real *I*, of who I am; I cannot imagine myself without them, because without them *I*

would not be I; and, of course, they are requirements for my happiness. [...] It is necessary to affirm life in what it has of human, plot-like, dramatic, projective; in short, *mine*. My life is mine, each one's; there is nothing that can be named as "life in general". The "other life" must be *my* other life. Not only "life", understood as a determinate species, because it is not about this, but with the characters that intrinsically belong to it. (Marías 1987, pp. 356 *and* 358, author's emphasis)[3]

The question now, of course, is to identify the elements of my circumstance that are not extrinsic but constitutive determinations of *my life* (each one's). According to Marías, there are two elements that form part of my circumstance and which are constitutive determinations of *my life*, inasmuch as without them *my life* would no longer be the *same* concrete reality it is now. Since they are *constitutive* circumstantial elements of *my life*, they are included in the kind of indefinite perdurance that *my life* intrinsically postulates. These constitutive circumstantial elements are two. First, that concrete and precise personal reality whom I found *radicated* in *my life* as being part of my circumstance and with whom I am in love. Second, the kind of worldly corporeal installation in which *my life* already happens to be realised and which gives *my life* its empirical concreteness as that concrete *man* I am and not another.

Marías's claim that the kind of indefinite perdurance that *my life* (each one's) intrinsically postulates involves other personal realities—that is, other *lives* which are not *my life*—is interesting inasmuch as it shows that even while strictly speaking what is postulated is the indefinite

---

[3] My translation. The original Spanish text reads: "[...] la otra vida [...] hay que interpretarla como *otro acto del drama*; se entiende, del *mismo* drama que es mi vida. La circunstancialidad de la vida humana impone ciertamente, tras la muerte, una pérdida de la circunstancia mundana, un paso a otra—es lo que siempre se ha llamado 'el otro mundo'; pero esta pérdida tiene que ser *parcial*. En esta vida, siempre llevo conmigo parte de mi circunstancia, aunque esta cambie constantemente en su conjunto. Ciertamente esto no se puede aplicar literalmente si se trata de la otra vida, del otro mundo, pero si *yo soy yo y mi circunstancia* (no solamente 'tengo' circunstancia o soy circunstancial) hay ingredientes de ella que me constituyen esencialmente mi vida, que son ingredientes de mi *yo* real, de quien soy; no me puedo imaginar sin ellos, porque sin ellos *no sería yo*; y, por supuesto, son requisitos de mi felicidad. [...] Es menester la afirmación de la vida en lo que tiene de humano, argumental, dramático, proyectivo; en suma, *mío*. Mi vida es mía, la de cada cual; no hay nada que pueda llamarse 'vida en general'. La 'otra vida' tiene que ser *mi* otra vida. No solamente 'vida', entendida como una especie determinada, porque no se trata de esto, sino con los caracteres que intrínsicamente le pertenecen".

perdurance of *my life* (each one's), this indefinite perdurance is far from being solipsistic. Marías's argument in this regard is still exclusively philosophical, grounded in the premises of his Metaphysical Anthropology and more concretely in his own conception of "being in love" ("*enamoramiento*"). The argument aims to show that there is a very precise and concrete personal reality who is not *my life* but who is nonetheless a constitutive element of my circumstance—and so without whom *my life* would no longer be the same concrete reality it is now—and also that the kind of worldly corporeal installation in which *my life* already happens to be realised, and that of the person with whom I am in love, are constitutive elements of my circumstance—inasmuch as, as will be explained next, without the same kind of worldly corporeal installation that constitutive determination which is my being in love with that person will be lost.

The starting point of Marías's argument in this regard is his affirmation that "being in love" is what in his Metaphysical Anthropology is named as an *installation*. As already explained in Chap. 3, this means that my (each one's) being in love shapes the concrete way in which I *live* my whole reality—in Marías's words:

> [...] being in love affects what he [*man*] is, in that radical form we have called *installation*. The fact is that while other installations—sex, age, race, class, language—are of a generic or collective natura, the installation represented by being in love is a strictly individual and personal condition: installed in my being-in-love with a certain woman, I project myself vectorially from that love and live *all* reality out of it. (Marías 1970a, p. 195, author's emphasis [Marías 1970b, p. 229])

I cannot be in love without being in love with a concrete person. This is an obvious conceptual requirement of what being in love means, and suffices to show that my being in love *intrinsically* refers to that concrete person with whom I am in love. Since, according to Marías, my being in love is an installation and as such constitutively shapes my own whole living, my installation of being in love should be preserved in its concrete form in order that *my life* does not lose its current concreteness—that is, in order that *my life* remains being the *same life* it is now. Therefore, my installation of being in love, in the concrete form in which it happens to be realised in *my life*, is also included in the kind of indefinite perdurance that *my life* (each one's) intrinsically postulates. Now, given that my being in love intrinsically refers to that concrete person with whom I am in love, the indefinite perdurance of that concrete person is therefore also postulated by *my life*—inasmuch as without that concrete person I would no longer be installed in my being in love and so my whole living would drastically change to the point of it no longer being *my* living. In other words, and to put it more succinctly, Marías's argument can be stated as follows: my being in love is an installation which constitutively shapes my whole living and so without which *my life* as *radical reality* loses its concreteness, therefore *my life* postulates the indefinite perdurance of my being in love; my being in love intrinsically refers to that concrete person with whom I am in love; taking the two claims together, it follows that *my life* intrinsically postulates the indefinite perdurance of that person with whom I am in love.

My being in love is therefore an installation of *my life* which intrinsically refers to a very precise part of my circumstance—that is, to that concrete person with whom I am in love. My falling in love with that concrete person and not another may be a contingent event in my biography, but once I am in love with that concrete person, she becomes a constitutive determination of *my life*. That person with whom I am in love is a personal reality on her own, and I recognise her and love her as such, but strictly speaking that person is to me a *radicated reality* of *my life* whom I discover as her being part of my circumstance. My worldly installation is corporeal—meaning that the way I am in this world and relate to it is through this precise concrete body which I call "my body". The way I discover and relate to the person with whom I am in love is therefore through my (and her) corporeal worldly installation. So, despite actually recognising that the person with whom I am in love is a personal reality on her own, I deal with her not as her just being a personal reality but as her being a *corporeal personal reality*—that is, and to put it in more formal terms, my apprehension of that personal reality with whom I am in love, and my relation with her, is *intrinsically* mediated by her (and my) worldly corporeal installation. I cannot be in love with a concrete person without also being in love with her body because I cannot relate to, or in fact have any apprehension at all of that person stripped of her concrete corporeal installation. My being in love with a concrete person therefore *intrinsically* involves my being in love with her (or his) body. Marías summarises this argument in the following quote from *Antropología metafísica*:

> Man and woman fall in love bodily because they live bodily, because the body is the place where the person shows himself and becomes present; it is there that we find him. But it would be a mistake to believe that bodies fall in love with each other; we do not even—though this would seem more plausible—fall in love with a body. We fall in love with a *person*, who is certainly corporeal; and then we love *that person's* body, precisely as *her* body, because it is hers (or his). (Marías 1970a, p. 197, author's emphasis [Marías 1970b, p. 231])

According to Marías, therefore, my being in love *intrinsically* involves my being in love with the body of that person with whom I am in love. If I were to lose my worldly corporeal installation, or if that person with whom I am in love were to lose hers, my installation of being in love would also be lost—and since the installation of being in love is a constitutive determination of *my life* which shapes my own whole living, this means that *my life* would lose its concreteness and so would no longer be the *same life*. This is what leads Marías to conclude that my worldly corporeal installation, and that of the person with whom I am in love, are constitutive elements of my circumstance without which *my life* will lose its concreteness, and which are therefore included in the kind of indefinite perdurance that *my life* intrinsically postulates. Marías makes this claim explicit in his *La felicidad humana*:

> Remember that I usually define the human person as *someone corporeal*, someone and not something, person and not thing, yes, but corporeal. This is how we encounter human reality, how we recognise it, how we live it, how we love it. Let us leave aside that it could live in another form, what we understand by human person is the corporeal, carnal person. And this is precisely the object of love. No one loves a body; we love someone, yes, but that someone is carnal. [...] In the human reality of love, corporeality is essential, and this is why the pretension of perduration after death can-

not lose that character. The loved person is corporeal and carnal, and we do not know how to imagine her otherwise. This does not mean that the person is her body, not at all, she is a "you" of who that body is, but she is an incarnated "you", corporeally realised. That is precisely the human condition. (Marías 1987, p. 348, author's emphasis)[4]

In *Antropología metafísica*, Marías points out that "worldhood" ("*mundanidad*")—that is, circumstantiality: the claim that there is a world (circumstance) with which I happen to coexist and relate to—is an a priori necessarily requirement for *my life* (each one's), and as such pertains to the *analytical structure of human life*. "Worldhood" is straightforwardly inferred from Ortega's formula that "*Yo soy yo y mi circumstancia*" ("I am myself and my circumstance"). However, and according to Marías, the fact that I am corporeal, and therefore that the way I relate to my circumstance is through corporeality and more concretely through this body, which I call "my body" despite strictly speaking it not being a *thing* which I possess, is an anthropological determination and as such pertains to the *empirical structure of human life*. On the premises of Marías's Metaphysical Anthropology, this means that there is no contradiction in allowing the possibility of variation regarding the concrete worldly installation in which *my life* (each one's) already happens to be realised. More generally, it implies that there is no a priori reason for denying that *human life* may be realised in a worldly installation different to that of *man*, either embodied or disembodied, but always provided that it is still circumstantial (see: Marías 1970a, pp. 97–98 [Marías 1970b, pp. 117–118]).

As already explained in Chap. 4, the conceptual distinction between *biological death* and *personal death*, together with Marías's claim that corporeality is an *anthropological* installation and so is not an a priori

---

[4] My translation. The original Spanish text reads: "Recuérdese que suelo definir a la persona humana como *alguien corporal*, alguien y no algo, persona y no cosa, sí, pero corporal. Así encontramos la realidad humana, así la reconocemos, la vivimos, la amamos. Dejemos de lado que pudiera vivir de otra forma, lo que entendemos por persona humana es la persona corporal, carnal. Y este es precisamente el objeto del amor. Nadie ama a un cuerpo; se ama a alguien, sí, pero ese alguien es carnal. [...] En la realidad humana del amor, la corporeidad es esencial, y por eso la pretensión de perduración tras la muerte no puede perder ese carácter. La persona amada es corpórea y carnal, y no sabemos imaginarle de otro modo. Esto no quiere decir que la persona sea su cuerpo, en modo alguno, es un 'tú' de quien es ese cuerpo, pero es un 'tu' encarnado, corpóreamente realizado. Esa es precisamente la condición humana".

necessary requirement for *my life* but an empirical determination of it that may therefore vary, allows Marías to show the conceptual possibility that *my life* (each one's) may perdure after my *biological death* occurs. Once this distinction is made, there seems to be no conceptual reason for denying the possibility that *my life* may continue after my *biological death*—inasmuch as there is no a priori conceptual reason for denying the possibility that after the loss of my current concrete worldly corporeal installation, *my life* may be realised (better said, transformed) on another concrete *empirical structure*. Now, Marías's claim that the kind of indefinite perdurance that *my life* (each one's) intrinsically postulates involves the preservation of my worldly corporeal installation (and that of the person with whom I am in love) implies that despite *human life* being conceivable under different types of worldly installation, the kind of indefinite perdurance that *my life* (each one's) intrinsically postulates refers to the same worldly corporeal installation in which *my life* already happens to be realised in this my earthly living—otherwise *my life* would no longer be the *same life,* inasmuch as if I were to lose my current worldly corporeal installation I would then lose my installation of being in love, and this installation of being in love is a constitutive determination of *my life* without which *my life* would no longer be the same concrete reality it is now.

Let me emphasise that Marías's claim that my (and that of the person with whom I am in love) worldly corporeal installation is a constitutive circumstantial determination of *my life* does not preclude the possibility of the perdurance of *my life* (each one's) after my *biological death* occurs—although it certainly adds an important condition for this perdurance. As already explained in Chap. 4, *biological death* is defined as the loss of my (each one his own) current concrete worldly corporeal installation—that is, the annihilation of this concrete body which I call "my body" and through which I deal with my circumstance. *Biological death* necessarily implies therefore a *numerical* change in my worldly installation. In claiming that *my life* (each one's) intrinsically postulates the indefinite perdurance of the same kind of worldly corporeal installation in which *my life* (each one's) already happens to be realised, Marías is not denying the possibility of variation regarding my worldly installation—after all, and as just explained, while "worldhood" (that is, circumstantiality) is an a priori necessary requirement without which there cannot be any *human life*, and so pertaining to the *analytical structure of human life*, the concrete way in which worldhood is realised is still an empirical determination of *my life* that may therefore vary. Marías is therefore not denying the possibility that my (each one's) worldly installation varies after my *biological death* occurs. Rather, what he is arguing is that this variation, if it were to occur, and there is no conceptual reason for denying the possibility that it may occur, even while necessarily implying a *numerical change* in my worldly corporeal installation, should nonetheless preserve the *same kind* of worldly corporeal installation in which *my life* (each one's) already happens to be realised—at least if it is to satisfy the ontological postulate intrinsic to *my life* (each one's) regarding its own indefinite perdurance. In other words, and to put it more concisely, Marías's claim that the kind of indefinite perdurance that *my life* (each one's) intrinsically postulates involves the indefinite perdurance of my corporeal worldly installation (and that of the person with whom I am in love) does not preclude the possibility of this indefinite perdurance even when my *biological death* consists in the loss of my (each one his own) current *concrete corporeal worldly installation*, inasmuch as there is still no conceptual reason for denying the possibility that after my *biological death* occurs, *my life* could then be transformed into another concrete corporeal worldly installation which, despite necessarily being *numerically distinct* from my concrete current worldly corporeal installation, may still be *qualitatively similar* to it.

Therefore, and according to Marías, in addition to the *who* I am, the executive I, *my life* (each one's) intrinsically postulates the indefinite perdurance of that precise person with whom I am in love, and the indefinite perdurance—in qualitative, non-numerical terms—of my worldly corporeal installation (and that of the person with whom I am in love). Marías's argumentation in this regard has been exclusively philosophical, inferred from the premises of his Metaphysical Anthropology, and more concretely from his conception of being in love as an installation which shapes my (each one's) whole living—and which therefore should be considered as a constitutive determination of *my life* without which *my life* will lose its concreteness. Up to this point, Marías's discussion on the "other life" has not involved any sort of reference to any religious or theological claim—related either to Christianity or to God or to religion in a more general and vague sense.

From now on, Marías's argumentation explicitly focuses on Christian Salvation through Resurrection, as announced and said to be exemplified by Jesus Christ. It is now, therefore, that the shift from the exclusively philosophical argumentative level to Marías's own interpretation of the contents of Christian Revelation occurs.

Marías rightly points out that Christian Salvation through Resurrection is the only kind of indefinite perdurance after my *biological death* occurs that would satisfy the ontological postulate intrinsic to *my life* (each one's) regarding its own indefinite perdurance. This is so because the kind of indefinite existence involved in Christian Salvation through Resurrection claims the indefinite perdurance of *my life* (each one's) in its concreteness, as it continuing to be the *same* concrete *life* that it already is. More precisely, the kind of indefinite existence involved after Christian Resurrection claims to preserve a qualitatively similar worldly corporeal installation to that in which *my life* already happens to be realised; and more generally claims to be a *continuation* of my (each one's) earthly living—and all this without having to deny the anthropological necessity of *biological death,* but rather presupposing it as a necessary pre-condition without which Salvation could not occur. Marías does not explicitly state this argument in his *Antropología metafísica*, in which as already mentioned he generally sticks to the philosophical level of his argumentation, but it is clearly formulated in his later works, and especially in his *La felicidad humana*:

> For the most part of history there has been a conception of survival that we might call "residual". By waiting for some kind of immortality, it has often been thought that something remains—*non omnis morias*, I will not die completely. It is aspired to that there will be a remainder, sometimes simply the fame or the name, in other cases something personal. In this way, a conception of immortality is reached that is literally "fleshless" ["*descarnada*"]—in short, spectral. Remember the words of Achilles, king of the dead, who would prefer to be the servant of the last peasant with a whole-body, full life. In Christianity, of course, it is not posited in this way, although it is not infrequent that within it tendencies to the spectral or spirited resprout. At the very centre of the Christian hope for immortality

there is the Resurrection of the flesh; and I insist on the expression "of the flesh", because if the Resurrection "of the dead" is said, then a lot of clarity is lost: the dead could resurrect in many ways. Christ resurrects in His flesh, with His body, His wounds that can be touched, His voice, His gestures, His way of splitting bread. In the Ascension, Christ corporeally ascends into Heaven by His own power, and in the Assumption of the Virgin the corporeality of Hers is also brought into Heaven by a divine action. In the Christian conception there is no place for a residual or spectral image of immortality of this kind. It is, then, about a *corporeal* and *worldly* life. The other world is talked about—all other that you want, but world—the "new Jerusalem". "I saw a new heaven and a new earth", says Saint John. It would be about, and this is what we should try to understand, a human life with *another empirical structure*; not what might be another species, another type of reality, because it is *my life*, each one's, the one that would have to exist with this new structure. Instead of looking for a remnant or residue, something that simply remains or is saved, we must try to methodically suppress the limitations and thus imagine other life as it being a dilatation of this one, as it being a fullness without deficiencies. (Marías 1987, pp. 360–361, author's emphasis)[5]

---

[5] My translation. The original Spanish text reads: "Durante la mayor parte de la historia ha habido una concepción de la pervivencia que podríamos llamar 'residual'. Al esperar algún tipo de inmortalidad, se ha solido pensar que algo queda: *non omnis morias*, no moriré del todo. Se aspira a que quede algún resto, a veces simplemente la fama o el nombre, en otros casos algo personal. Así se llega a una concepción de la inmortalidad literalmente 'descarnada', en definitiva espectral. Recuérdense las palabras de Aquiles, rey de los muertos, que preferiría ser el siervo del último labrador con una vida plena, de cuerpo entero. En el cristianismo, por supuesto, la cosa no se plantea así, aunque dentro de él rebroten no pocas veces tendencias a lo espectral o espiritado. En el centro mismo de la esperanza cristiana de la inmortalidad está la resurrección de la carne; e insisto en la expresión 'de la carne', porque si se dice la resurrección 'de los muertos' se pierde mucha claridad: los muertos podrían resucitar de muchas maneras. Cristo resucita en su carne, con su cuerpo, sus heridas que se pueden tocar, su voz, sus gestos, su manera de partir el pan. En la Ascensión, Cristo asciende corporalmente a los cielos por su propio poder, y en la Asunción de la Virgen también la corporeidad de esta es llevada al cielo por una acción divina. En la concepción cristiana no hay lugar para esa imagen residual o espectral de la inmortalidad. Se trata, pues, de una vida *corporal* y *mundana*. Se habla del otro mundo—todo lo otro que se quiera, pero mundo—, de la 'nueva Jerusalén'. 'Vi un cielo nuevo y una tierra nueva', dice San Juan. Se trataría, y es lo que habría que intentar comprender, de una vida humana con *otra estructura empírica*; pero no lo que pudiera ser otra especie, otro tipo de realidad, porque es *mi vida*, la de cada cual, la que habría de existir con esa nueva estructura. En lugar de buscar un resto o residuo, algo que simplemente quede o se salve, hay que intentar metódicamente suprimir las limitaciones y así imaginar otra vida como una dilatación de esta, como una plenitud sin deficiencias".

Marías makes a similar claim in his *La perspectiva cristiana*. There he emphasises again that Christian Salvation through Resurrection does not deny but in fact presupposes the anthropological necessity of *biological death*, while still claiming the indefinite perdurance of *my life* (each one's) in a numerically different but nonetheless qualitatively similar corporeal worldly installation to the one in which *my life* already happens to be realised in this my earthly living:

> And Christianity speaks not only of the Resurrection of the dead, but of the *flesh*. This cannot be overlooked. It is about the Salvation of the whole reality, just as it is. [...] The Christian Resurrection is of the *flesh*, not simply of the dead, which could occur in other ways. But it is Resurrection "from among the dead"—that is, after death, without avoiding it. (Marías 1999b, p. 81, author's emphasis)[6]

Christian Salvation through Resurrection appears therefore as the only way in which my (each one's) *human* reality could be fulfilled—inasmuch as only if Christian Salvation through Resurrection were to occur would the ontological postulate intrinsic to *my life* (each one's) regarding its own indefinite perdurance be satisfied. Since according to Marías, and as already explained in Chap. 4, my (each one's) conscious hope for the indefinite perdurance of *my life* (each one's) is justified as it being a conscious endorsement of my own *human* reality, his claim that only if Christian Salvation through Resurrection were to occur would *my life* perdure indefinitely implies that my (each one's) conscious hope for Christian Salvation is likewise justified as it being a conscious endorsement of my (each one's) ultimate *human* reality—*mediately*, as Christian Salvation through Resurrection being the only way to guarantee the indefinite perdurance of *my life* (each one's).

---

[6] My translation. The original Spanish text reads: "Y el cristianismo no habla sólo de la resurrección de los muertos, sino de la *carne*. No se puede pasar por alto esto. Se trata de la salvación de la realidad entera, tal como es. [...] La resurrección cristiana es de la *carne*, no simplemente de los muertos, lo que podría ser de otras maneras. Pero es resurrección 'de entre los muertos', es decir, después de la muerte, sin escamotearla".

Marías's argumentation of course requires taking Christian Salvation through Resurrection as an open possibility which therefore might perhaps occur, since one cannot hope for what one considers impossible. However, neither does Marías's argumentation require or imply accepting that in fact God does actually exist or that He is going to save us through Resurrection. After all, Marías's argumentation refers to my (each one's) *human* reality, not to any alleged evidence for claiming the existence of God. Let me emphasise once more, since this is a crucial aspect, that Marías's argumentation is not, and does not aim to be, an argument for proving the *truth* (nor even the likelihood) of the factual claim that God actually exists or that Salvation through Resurrection will, as a matter of fact, actually occur. Rather, Marías's argumentation aims to show that my (each one's) conscious hope for Christian Salvation through Resurrection is a legitimate reaction of mine, inasmuch as it not only is consistent with but amounts to a conscious endorsement of my own ultimate *human* nature.

However, despite neither presupposing nor implying accepting as a truth the factual claim that God exists, the mere reference to Christian Salvation through Resurrection transformed Marías's argumentation thereafter into a *religious* argumentation. This is so because not just its alleged truth but our mere awareness of the possibility that Christian Salvation through Resurrection could actually occur is exclusively attained from Christian Revelation—and, more concretely, from the Biblical testimony on the *biography* of that personal (and divine) reality who is said to be Jesus Christ and of whom it is said, among other things, to be the Son of God and that He died and later resurrected to proclaim and show the opportunity of Salvation to each and every man. The so to say real or factual possibility that Christian Salvation through Resurrection could actually occur is exclusively founded on the hypothetical possibility that Jesus Christ did actually resurrect—and, here comes the crucial point, that Jesus Christ resurrected is a *fact* that is seen; that is, an object of Revelation, and not a philosophical premise to be demonstrated through philosophical reasoning. The possibility that Christian Resurrection could actually occur is therefore ultimately indemonstrable, since it

depends on the hypothetical possibility that Jesus Christ did actually resurrect, which is a *fact* and as such is not, and cannot be, inferred from any
philosophical premise—which, as Marías points out, is already clearly
illustrated in the Biblical testimony in reference to Paul the Apostle and
his visit to Athens. The Athenian philosophers were eager to listen to Paul
the Apostle about the new religion which was Christianity, but when he
mentioned the Resurrection of the dead the philosophers mocked him
and stopped listening (Acts 17: 16–34). In *La perspectiva cristiana*, the
claim that the possibility that Christian Salvation through Resurrection
could actually occur is not a philosophical premise to be demonstrated
through philosophical reasoning but an object of Revelation, exclusively
founded in the hypothetical possibility that Jesus Christ did actually resurrect, is made explicit in the following quote:

> [...] the *Resurrection*. This is rationally inaccessible, of course indemon-
> strable, an object of *Revelation*. Its foundation is that of Christ, which
> exemplifies it and shows it, makes it accessible before the apostles and espe-
> cially before Thomas, who is not present when Jesus appears to the others,
> who does not quite believe what *they tell him*, but as soon as he *sees it*—that
> is, when he is in the situation of the others—he recognises it in the most
> energetic and admirable way: "My Lord and my God!". I have always
> thought that Saint Thomas the Apostle should be the patron saint of phi-
> losophers. The Resurrection—let us insist, inaccessible to reason and
> incomprehensible to the Greeks—is *essential nucleus* of Christianity,
> founded on that of Christ and promised by Him to all men. (Marías
> 1999b, pp. 80–81, author's emphasis)[7]

Marías's argumentation is not, and does not aim to be, an argument
for proving the *truth* (nor even the likelihood) of the factual claim that

---

[7] My translation. The original Spanish text reads: "[...] la *resurrección*. Esta es racionalmente inaccesible, por supuesto indemostrable, objeto de *revelación*. Su fundamento es la de Cristo, que la
ejemplifica y la muestra, la hace accesible, ante los apóstoles y muy particularmente ante Tomás,
que no estaba presente cuando Jesús se aparece a los demás, que no acaba de creer lo que *le dicen*,
pero tan pronto como *lo ve*—es decir, cuando está en la situación de los demás—, lo reconoce de la
forma más enérgica y admirable: '¡Señor mío y Dios mío!'. Siempre he pensado que Santo Tomás
apóstol debería ser patrono de los filósofos. La resurrección, inaccesible a la razón, insistamos en
ello, incomprensible para los griegos, es *núcleo esencial* del cristianismo, fundada en la de Cristo y
prometida por él a todos los hombres".

Christian Salvation through Resurrection will, as a matter of fact, actually occur—precisely because such a claim is ultimately indemonstrable, exclusively founded in Christian Revelation. However, and despite Marías seemingly not explicitly formulating this line of reasoning, his argumentation offers a way to justify my (each one's) hope that Jesus Christ did as a matter of fact actually resurrect, and more generally my hope for Christian Revelation to be true. As just explained, the real or factual possibility that Christian Salvation could actually occur is exclusively grounded in Christian Revelation, and more concretely in the hypothetical possibility that Jesus Christ did actually resurrect. This means that I cannot hope for Christian Salvation through Resurrection to occur without also hoping that Christian Revelation is true—that is, without hoping that Jesus Christ did actually resurrect. In other words, my hope for Christian Salvation through Resurrection *presupposes* my hope for Christian Revelation to be true. Therefore, if Marías is right in that my (each one's) hope for Christian Salvation through Resurrection is justified, then my hope that Christian Revelation is true would in principle also be justified—inasmuch as it is not possible to hope for Christian Salvation through Resurrection without also hoping for Christian Revelation to be true.

Traditionally, the most common position among Christians is to justify hope for Christian Salvation through Resurrection in terms of a previous hope for the truth of Christian Revelation. That is, the most common position is to claim that my hope that Jesus Christ did actually resurrect is what sustains my hope that I, and each and all man, will enjoy of God's Salvation. Marías's argumentation is interesting in this regard because it offers the possibility of going in the opposite direction—it is my hope in the indefinite perdurance of *my life*, and so my hope for Christian Salvation through Resurrection to actually occur, that grounds my hope that Jesus Christ did actually resurrect, and more generally my hope that Christian Revelation is true.

Let me emphasise that this hope for Christian Revelation to be true neither requires nor implies affirming the truth of Christian Revelation—to put it more formally, I am justified in hoping that Jesus Christ did actually resurrect but this hope of mine does not constitute any sort of evidence for the factual claim that Jesus Christ did actually resurrect. This is so because, as already mentioned, Marías's argumentation refers to my (each one's) own ultimate *human* constitutive condition, involving no reference to any alleged evidence for claiming the truth, or even the likelihood, of the contents of Christian Revelation—my hope for Christian Revelation to be true is founded in my hope for Christian Salvation through Resurrection to occur, which in its turn is founded in my hope that the ontological postulate intrinsic to *my life* (each one's) referring to its own indefinite perdurance would be satisfied. However, even when Marías's argumentation does not justify affirming the truth of Christian Revelation, it nonetheless preserves a traditional understanding of Christian Revelation—that is, as it being a description of divinely founded facts that are said to have actually occurred. In other words, even while I have no evidential justification for affirming the truth of Christian Revelation, what I hope for is that Christian Revelation is actually true. Marías's argumentation, therefore, has the important merit of justifying my hope that Christian Revelation be true without relying on any alleged evidence for its truth, and without thereby having to deny its evidential or factual content.

Since the possibility that Christian Salvation through Resurrection could as a matter of fact actually occur is a *religious* claim, exclusively grounded in Christian Revelation and therefore lacking of philosophical justification, there may perhaps be philosophical reasons contradicting this possibility and so contravening my (each one's) conscious hope for it. In this regard, and to begin with, it should be noted that, on the premises of Marías's Metaphysical Anthropology, there is no conceptual reason for denying the conceptual possibility of Christian Resurrection. On the one hand, there is nothing incoherent in claiming the possibility that *my life* (each one's) may be realised or transformed into another *empirical structure*, always provided that the a priori necessary requirements referred to in the *analytical structure of human life* are met. On the other hand, Christian Salvation through Resurrection does not deny but actually assumes as a pre-condition the anthropological necessity of *biological death*. Therefore, and at least at first sight, the possibility of Christian Salvation through Resurrection does not contradict the general premises of Marías's Metaphysical Anthropology.

However, while Christian Salvation through Resurrection may be a conceptual possibility, it may still be the case that Christian Resurrection, and Christian Revelation more generally, carries with it some anthropological views that may contradict that conception of *man*, and *human life* more generally, which according to Marías we find through philosophical reasoning—that is, it may be the case that the contents of Christian Revelation contradict the premises of Marías's Metaphysical Anthropology. To discover if this is the case, Marías carries out the task of analysing the meaning of Christian Revelation. As mentioned before, this is a *religious* analysis of Christian Revelation—that is, within religion, with no pretension of proving its truth but rather of understanding its *meaning*.

As a result of this religious analysis of Christian Revelation, the most systematic and exhaustive formulation of which, as already mentioned, is found in his book *La perspectiva cristiana*, Marías claims that Christianity does not just imply but actually ultimately consists in the conception of *man* as *person*. Man is conceived as an *incarnated* personal reality, *created* by God in his love and realised in His image and likeness (*imago Dei*). God is also conceived as a personal reality—and in the divine person of Jesus Christ, God is incarnated as *man*. God *is* love and He bears a personal, loving and paternal relationship with each and every man. Each and every man is unique and irreplaceable, with his own concreteness, but all men live in *fraternity*—that is, in *"convivencia"* ("living-with")—since they are all, without a single exception, sons of the same *Father* and therefore they are all *brothers*. Man does not choose to live, but once *his life* is given, he is free to live as he feels is most appropriate. Man is therefore responsible for his living—at all times he should decide, on his own, what to do. His earthly life is given in freedom so that he himself can choose the person, the *who*, he will be eternally in Heaven. Moreover, since man is made in the image and likeness of God, the presence of God is intrinsic to each and all men. This last claim has two important implications. First, that (partial and imperfect) apprehension of the reality of God can be found within oneself, through apprehension of my human— that is, personal—reality. Second, that any attempt at self-affirmation, of consciously endorsing my own human reality, whether I know it or not, is already an affirmation of God's reality—and the other way round, an affirmation of God is a self-affirming exercise regarding my (each one's) human reality. Overall, and this is important to note, the claim that man is made in the image and likeness of God shows that Marías's approach when aiming to justify my (each one's) conscious hope for Christian Salvation through Resurrection, and with it my hope that Christian Revelation is true, by appealing to my own (each one's) *human* reality does not contravene but is actually in line with the contents of Christian Revelation.

None of these *religious* claims contradicts the *philosophical* claims involved in Marías's Metaphysical Anthropology—actually, in general lines they seem to coincide. Marías condenses his own religious interpretation of Christian Revelation in the following quote from *La perspectiva cristiana*, in which he comes to the conclusion that "if this is *thought* about, an *anthropology* of the human person is made; if this is lived, one is simply a Christian":

> Christianity *consists* of the vision of man as person. It has not been "thought" in this way, it has only begun to be done, still in a very insufficient way, because what has been thought about that reality that we are is strangely scarce; but Christianity has *lived* this whenever it has been faithful to itself, and every Christian, even the least "theoretical" or "intellectual", lives his religion *personally* if it is sincere and part of his life. What is surprising is the coherence of these "elementary" experiences, accessible to all, with what philosophical thought discovers when approaching the notion of person. The Christian sees himself as an unmistakable *someone*, not "something", but a "who" distinct from all "what", with proper *name, created* and loved by God, not alone and isolated but in *living-with* ["*convivencia*"] those who, for being sons of the same Father, are *brothers*. He feels *free* and, therefore, *responsible*, capable of choice and decision with a received reality of which he is not the author, but which is *his own*. He knows he is capable of *repentance*, of turning to his own reality—of accepting or rejecting it and of correcting it. And that reality is *projective*, it consists in anticipation of the future—in what he is going to do, in who he intends to be—and it is loving—defined by affection towards some persons and the duty to extend it to all the rest. And he aspires to perdurance, to continue living after the inevitable death—not an isolated perdurance but with the others; he prays his belief in the "communion of the saints". By his loving condition he lives the possibility of the *interpenetration* of other persons, of being "inhabited"

by some of them. If this is *thought* about, an *anthropology* of the human person is made; if this is lived, one is simply a Christian. (Marías 1999b, pp. 119–120, author's emphasis)[8]

There is, therefore, and according to Marías, no philosophical impediment to consciously hoping for Christian Salvation through Resurrection. Hence, my (each one's) conscious hope for Christian Salvation through Resurrection remains justified as it being a conscious endorsement of my own *human* reality, inasmuch as only if this Salvation were to occur would the ontological postulate intrinsic to *my life* (each one's) regarding its own indefinite perdurance be satisfied.

Now, Marías argues, once the possibility of Christian Salvation through Resurrection is embraced as the object of my (each one's) hope, the analysis of Christian Revelation allows me to *imagine*, in a more concrete and therefore vivid way, the kind of indefinite perdurance I may hopefully enjoy after my *biological death* occurs. These inferences from Christian Revelation may shape the content of my hope, but they are not, and Marías does not intend them to be, evidences for the *truth* of any religious statement, not even that regarding the factual claim that God actually exists and that He will save us through Resurrection—again, they are inferences from the contents of Christian Revelation, and so within religion, on its assumption and with no pretension of proving its truth.

---

[8] My translation. The original Spanish text reads: "El cristianismo *consiste* en la visión del hombre como persona. No se lo ha 'pensado' así, solamente se ha empezado a hacerlo, todavía de manera muy insuficiente, porque es extrañamente escaso lo que se ha pensado sobre esa realidad que somos; pero el cristianismo lo ha *vivido* siempre que ha sido fiel a sí mismo, y cada cristiano, aun el menos 'teórico' o 'intelectual', vive *personalmente* su religión si esta es sincera y forma parte de su vida. Lo sorprendente es la coherencia de esas vivencias 'elementales', accesibles a todos, con lo que el pensamiento filosófico descubre al acercarse a la noción de persona. El cristiano se ve a sí mismo como *alguien* inconfundible, no 'algo', un 'quién' distinto de todo 'qué', con *nombre* propio, *creado* y amado por Dios, no solo y aislado, sino en *convivencia* con los que, por ser hijos del mismo Padre, son *hermanos*. Se siente *libre* y, por tanto, *responsable*, capaz de elección y decisión con una realidad recibida, de la que no es autor, pero *propia*. Se sabe capaz de *arrepentimiento*, de volver sobre la propia realidad, aceptarla o rechazarla y corregirla. Y esa realidad es *proyectiva*, consiste en anticipación del futuro, de lo que va a hacer, de quién pretende ser, y es amorosa, definida por la afección hacia algunas personas y el deber de que se extienda a las demás. Y aspira a la pervivencia, a seguir viviendo después de la muerte inevitable, no aislada sino con los demás—reza su creencia en la 'comunión de los santos'—. Vive su condición amorosa la posibilidad de la *interpenetración* de otras personas, de ser 'habitado' por algunas. Si esto se *piensa*, se hace una *antropología* de la persona humana; si se lo vive, se es simplemente cristiano".

According to Marías, and in addition to referring to an after *biological death* existence and preserving a not numerically identical but still qualitatively similar corporeal worldly installation to that in which *my life* (each one's) already happens to be realised, Christian Salvation through Resurrection involves two central claims. These two claims are central to the concept of Christian Salvation through Resurrection as found in Christian Revelation, and so should be considered when aiming to understand, and above all when trying to imagine with some degree of concreteness, the kind of indefinite perdurance involved in Christian Salvation. On the one hand, Christian Salvation through Resurrection involves the indefinite perdurance of *my life* after my *biological death* occurs as it continuing to be the *same* personal or biographical reality it already is right now—that is, the "other life", whatever the details of its concrete realisation may be and how differently it may be from *what* it is now, would still be *my life*: another act of the same dramatic reality that is *my life* and which would therefore be part of its plot. On the other hand, it is central to the concept of Christian Salvation that the indefinite perdurance involved in it implies either my supreme happiness or my supreme unhappiness, and that one or another possibility *somehow* depends on my (each one's) own earthly living. In Marías's words:

> Christianity starts from two fundamental notions: first, that the other life has to do with this one, that is, that it continues as the life of the same person; second, that such a denouement is extreme, the supreme happiness or the supreme unhappiness, and that to some extent depends on the person himself. (Marías 1999b, p. 74)[9]

These two claims, together with Marías's own conception of human happiness already discussed in Chap. 4, allows us to *imagine* in a vivid and concrete way the kind of indefinite perdurance that *might* be involved in Christian Salvation through Resurrection—if it were to occur, which strictly speaking we do not know, although we hope for it. If the "other

---

[9] My translation. The original Spanish text reads: "El cristianismo parte de dos nociones fundamentales: la primera, que la otra vida tiene que ver con esta, es decir, que la continúa como vida de la misma persona; en segundo lugar, que ese desenlace es extremo, la suma felicidad o la suma infelicidad, y que en alguna medida depende de la persona misma".

life" were to be the supreme form of happiness, and if Marías is right in that human happiness consists in the realisation of my vocation (each one his own), the "other life" might be imagined as the full realisation of my own vocation. More concretely, it could be imagined as the fulfilment of each and all of the trajectories in which my vocation (each one his own) would be realised but that I have been incapable of carrying out during my finite earthly living, either because external reasons have impeded it or simply because of the character of preferring and deferring intrinsic to living. The "other life" should also be imagined in communion with that precise concrete person with whom I am in love, since as explained before this person is an intrinsic part of my reality without whom I would no longer be the *who* I am, and so her company is an indispensable condition for my happiness—and, I add, it should also be imagined in communion with the persons who I love, even if strictly speaking I am not *in love with* them. If imagined in this way, the "other life" would still be *my life*, as it would be the continuation (and fulfilment) of its originary plot. In his *La felicidad humana*, Marías makes this point as follows:

> I have insisted at length, because it seems to me essential, that human life is composed of *trajectories* in plural, multiple trajectories, like an arborescence or a series of flow rates that come together in a river, or like a sky-rocket. These trajectories are realised or not, to varying degrees, going on dividing, fragmenting, interrupting, being abandoned, getting frustrated, sometimes violently. What we name "the trajectory of our life", the main trajectory, is incomprehensible without the others. And we have seen that the fundamental reason why happiness is impossible in this world is precisely this—the forced renunciation of many trajectories. Well, among these trajectories there are more or less authentic ones, in different degrees. And it can be thought that in the other life the *authentic* trajectories that have not been able to be realised will find their realisation. To take the clearest example, let us think of a trajectory cut short by a chance occurrence, by an accident: the painter who goes blind, the musician who goes deaf; this is a brutal interruption of a trajectory that can be authentic, and it implies a dose of unhappiness. Without going to that extreme, there are innumerable trajectories which, due to the circumstances, are not realised or stay initiated. If they were to be realised, it would then be possible to meet that which one has truly wanted to be and has not been able to be:

this would be the form of full happiness. The set of all the authentic trajectories would make up the plot of the enduring life, and this would be, at the same time, the true connection with personal life, with the who of each one, defined by his projects. I insisted before on the necessary connection of death with life. The connection of the other life with this one would precisely consist in the fulfillment or realisation of the authentic trajectories, of each one's true projects, the culmination of the deficient life of this world. (Marías 1987, pp. 367–368, author's emphasis; see also: Marías 1999a, pp. 84–87 [Marías 1999b, pp. 92–94])[10]

If imagined in this way, the kind of existence that I (each one) would enjoy if Christian Salvation through Resurrection were to occur would depend on my own living in this present earthly existence—inasmuch as it is now that I am making the originary plot of *my life*, the *who* I am and overall the *who* I want to be. In this way, the connection between "this" and the "other" life would be preserved, as both of them would be different acts of the same drama—so regardless of how they might differ, both would ultimately be *my life*. It is interesting to note that this is one of the few religious-related claims that Marías makes in his *Antropología metafísica*—although it is made there with no *explicit* mention of Christian Salvation through Resurrection. In the last two pages of

---

[10] My translation. The original Spanish text reads: "He insistido largamente, porque me parece esencial, en que la vida humana se compone de *trayectorias* en plural, múltiples, como una arborescencia o una serie de caudales que se juntan en un río, o un cohete. Esas trayectorias se realizan o no, más o menos, se van dividiendo, se fragmentan, se interrumpen, se abandonan, se frustran, a veces con violencia. Lo que llamamos, 'la trayectoria de nuestra vida', la trayectoria principal, es incomprensible sin las demás. Y hemos visto que la razón fundamental de que la felicidad sea imposible en este mundo es precisamente esa, la forzosa renuncia a muchas trayectorias. Pues bien, entre esas trayectorias las hay más o menos auténticas, en diferentes grados. Y se puede pensar que en la otra vida encontrarán su realización las trayectorias *auténticas* que no se han podido realizar. Para tomar el ejemplo más claro, pensemos en una trayectoria truncada por un azar, por un accidente: el pintor que se queda ciego, el músico sordo; es un corte brutal de una trayectoria que puede ser auténtica, y supone una dosis de infelicidad. Sin llegar a ese extremo, hay innumerables trayectorias que por las circunstancias no se realizan o quedan iniciadas. Si se realizaran, podría cumplirse lo que verdaderamente se ha querido ser y no se ha podido: esta sería la forma de la plena felicidad. El conjunto de todas las trayectorias auténticas compondría la trama de la vida perdurable, y esta sería, al mismo tiempo, la verdadera conexión con la vida personal, con el quién de cada uno, definido por sus proyectos. Insistí antes en la necesaria conexión de la muerte con la vida. Precisamente la conexión de la otra vida con esta consistiría en el cumplimiento o realización de las trayectorias auténticas, de los verdaderos proyectos de cada uno, la culminación de la deficiente vida de este mundo".

Antropología metafísica, Marías offers an argument as to why God *could not have* just created us directly in Heaven, thereby saving us from the deficiencies of earthly existence. I (each one) must make myself—that is, I myself alone, in my own way and under my own responsibility, must choose the *who* I want to be, what I want the plot of *my life* to be. This is why God could have not created me directly in Heaven, and why He gives freedom to my living—so that I myself on my own (each one of us) can freely choose the *person,* the *who,* I am going to be:

> If we are destined for another life without the internal conflicts of this one, and especially a life without this life's fleeting and transitory nature, without its inherent mortality, what is this life for? Could not God have placed us directly in the other, installed us once and for all in everlasting life? The idea that God "tests" us in this life, subjects us to a sort of moral examination to see how we behave before he rewards or punishes us, is too crude and unsatisfactory. What happens is this: if God had placed us directly in Paradise, we would be *something else.* Man is the being who, once created and placed in life, *makes himself.* And he makes himself projectively, and not only in his actual trajectory, the one we can tell of in his biography. Man makes himself in expectation, in dream, and in conflict; he makes himself out of his multiple installations, or better still out of the multiple dimensions of his unitary installation; he makes himself in authenticity and unauthenticity. Human life on earth is programmatic and at the same time always frustrated—that is why happiness is a necessary impossibility, that is why man needs to be happy and cannot be so. Mortal life—our numbered days—stretching between birth and death, is the time in which man *chooses* himself, not what he is but *who* he is, in which he invents and decides who he *wants to be* (and never fully becomes). We can imagine this life as the choice of the other life, the other as the realization of this life. One terrible verse in the *Dies Irae* has always moved me deeply, more than any other. It is the verse that says: *quidquid latet apparebit,* "all that is hidden will appear". All that has truly been wanted, will be. To this we condemn ourselves: to be, in truth and forever, what we have wished to be. (Marías 1970a, pp. 266–267, author's emphasis [Marías 1970b, pp. 308–309])

Each of us has his own vocation, and therefore we do not all aim at realising the same concrete trajectories. Moreover, we are not all in love with the same person—I am in love with some precise person but not another, and I am in love with her precisely because she is that precise person and not another. This means that there is no unique way to *imagine* the "other life". I guess this may be surprising to non-Christian philosophers and probably also to not a few Christian theologians. However, since each one of us is a unique personal reality with his own exclusive singularity, it follows from this that there cannot be a single way to imagine immortality, at least if it is to be fully and truly personal—and, let me add, within Christian faith, and regardless of what intellectualised theologians may claim, Salvation *should be* fully personal, just as the Resurrection of Jesus Christ is said to have been (and so to still be) fully personal. Personal immortality refers to the indefinite perdurance of *my life*, each one his own, and since no two lives are the same, there cannot be conceived two identical ways of being immortal.

In short, and to recap, Marías's argumentation consists in showing that my (each one's) conscious hope for Christian Salvation through Resurrection is justified as it being a conscious endorsement of my own *human* reality—and this is so because only if the Christian God were to exist and save us through Resurrection would the ontological postulate intrinsic to *my life* (each one's) referring to its own indefinite perdurance then be satisfied. The real or factual possibility that Christian Salvation through Resurrection could actually occur lacks of philosophical justification since it is exclusively grounded in Christian Revelation—and more concretely in the hypothetical possibility that Jesus Christ did, as a matter of fact, actually resurrect. However, there is no philosophical reason for denying that Christian Resurrection is conceptually possible. Moreover, neither does the way of conceiving personal reality involved in Christian Revelation contradict any philosophical claim—at least not those involved in Marías's Metaphysical Anthropology. In fact, they generally seem to coincide. There are, therefore, no philosophical reasons contravening my (each one's) conscious hope for Christian Salvation through Resurrection—hence my (each one's) conscious hope for Christian Salvation through Resurrection remains justified as it being a conscious endorsement of my own ultimate *human* reality, inasmuch as only if this Salvation were to occur would that ontological postulate intrinsic to *my life* (each one's) be satisfied. Although Marías does not seem to explicitly formulate this line of reasoning, from his argumentation it follows a way to justify my (each one's) hope that Christian Revelation is true without thereby having to affirm its being true—since it is not possible to hope for Christian Salvation through Resurrection without also hoping that Christian Revelation is true, if my hope for Christian Salvation through Resurrection is justified, then my hope that Christian Revelation is true is also justified.

To conclude, I would like to once again emphasise the importance of distinguishing between the two different argumentative levels involved in Marías's argumentation—on the one hand, Marías's philosophical reasoning related to the premises of his Metaphysical Anthropology; and on the other hand, Marías's religious interpretation of the contents of Christian Revelation. When reading Marías, and especially when reading the books published after *Antropología metafísica* such as *La felicidad humana*, a clear distinction should be made between the claims that are inferred from his Metaphysical Anthropology, and whose justification is therefore exclusively philosophical, and the claims that are inferred from Marías's analysis of the content of Christian Revelation, and which are therefore interpretative claims on Christian Revelation with no pretension of proving its *truth* but with the exclusive aim of understanding its meaning. Otherwise, Marías's intention may be easily misread as if he were trying to justify the possibility of Christian Salvation through Resurrection, and more generally the contents of Christian Revelation, on the basis of his Metaphysical Anthropology—which I suspect is nowadays the most common misinterpretation among scholars.

Let me explain this in a more detailed way. It is certain that Marías's analysis of the meaning of Christian Revelation leads him to conclude that Christian Salvation through Resurrection is conceptually possible. More generally, it leads him to conclude that the way of conceiving *man*, and *personal reality* more generally, implicit in Christian Revelation is not just consistent but largely coincides with the way of conceiving *man* and *human life* inferred through philosophical reasoning from his Metaphysical Anthropology. This consistency or even coincidence is relevant in Marías's argumentation inasmuch as it shows that there is no philosophical objection in my (each one's) conscious hope for Christian Salvation through Resurrection. Certainly, this coincidence seems to offer a way of arguing that the way of conceiving personal reality implicit in Christian Revelation is a correct *philosophical view*—at least provided we agree that Marías's Metaphysical Anthropology is a correct philosophical view. However, it offers no argument for demonstrating the properly religious content of Christianity, including the possibility that Christian Salvation through Resurrection could actually occur, which remains exclusively grounded in Revelation. We may agree that philosophical reasoning can show the conceptual possibility of Christian Salvation through Resurrection—that is, that such an event is neither self-contradictory nor in contradiction with other already established philosophical premises. However, the so to say real or factual possibility that, as a matter of fact, this Salvation could actually occur is still exclusively founded in the hypothetical possibility that Jesus Christ did actually resurrect—and of course that He did so to exemplify and announce to each and all men the opportunity of Salvation.

The crucial point is that the claim that Jesus Christ did actually resurrect is not a philosophical premise, but a factual claim related to a very precise biographical event in the life of that personal (and divine) reality who is said to be Jesus Christ. Philosophical reasoning alone cannot determine whether a concrete fact has actually occurred, although as I just said it can determine whether such a fact is conceptually possible—and, at least according to Marías, the fact that Jesus Christ did resurrect is a conceptual possibility inasmuch as it does not contradict any of the premises of his Metaphysical Anthropology. Therefore, and since the claim that Jesus Christ did actually resurrect is not a philosophical premise but a factual claim related to the biographical content of that precise personal (and divine) reality who is said to be Jesus Christ, it cannot be *demonstrated* by philosophical reasoning but can only be *apprehended narratively*, through the biography of Jesus Christ—that is, through the study and interpretation of Christian Revelation as we find it in the Biblical testimony. This is why, and despite starting from the philosophical premises of his Metaphysical Anthropology, Marías's argumentation with regard to my (each one's) conscious hope for Christian Salvation through Resurrection is ultimately a *religious argumentation*. It relies on accepting beforehand not just the conceptual possibility but the hypothetical possibility (but, let me emphasise, not its truth) that as a matter of fact Jesus Christ could actually have resurrected and that He did so to exemplify and announce to each and all men the opportunity of Salvation through Resurrection—and, let me say it again, the hypothetical possibility that Jesus Christ could have actually resurrected is not discovered through philosophical reasoning, but only found in Christian Revelation. Certainly, Marías's argumentation offers a way to justify my (each one's) hope that Christian Revelation is true without thereby having to affirm its truth, although it still requires prior acceptance of its hypothetical possibility.

Let me emphasise that, strictly speaking, this is not a deficiency of Marías's argumentation. In fact, it is quite the contrary. Once we realise that the real or factual possibility that Christian Salvation through Resurrection could actually occur relies not just on its conceptual possibility but on the hypothetical possibility that Jesus Christ did as a matter of fact actually resurrect, we should conclude that there is no, and there cannot be, any philosophical argument demonstrating the truth or even the likelihood that this Salvation will (or may) actually occur. Philosophy cannot determine whether Jesus Christ did actually resurrect—simply because this is not a philosophical claim that can be inferred from any given premise, but rather a biographical claim referring to a very precise event in that personal (and divine) reality who is said to be Jesus Christ. Marías's argumentation assumes the hypothetical possibility that Jesus Christ did actually resurrect, but it is important to emphasise that it neither presupposes nor claims to demonstrate either its truth or its likelihood—precisely because such an event is indemonstrable. Herein relies one of the main virtues of Marías's argumentation—in its offering a coherent way to justify my (each one's) conscious hope for Christian Salvation through Resurrection on the grounds of its hypothetical possibility and with no intention of demonstrating, precisely because it is indemonstrable, either the truth or the likelihood that this Salvation will actually occur. From a philosophical point of view, this is a virtue of Marías's argumentation because it respects the boundaries of philosophical reasoning—it does not require philosophy to demonstrate what it cannot demonstrate. From a Christian point of view, this is a virtue inasmuch as it succeeds in preserving the foundational role of the Biblical testimony about the Resurrection of Jesus Christ together with its revealed, and thereby indemonstrable, character.

References

Marías, J. (1970a) 1971. *Metaphysical Anthropology: The Empirical Structure of Human Life*. Trans. Frances M. López-Morillas. Pennsylvania: The Pennsylvania State University Press.

Marías, J. (1970b). *Antropología metafísica: la estructura empírica de la vida humana*. Madrid: Revista de Occidente.

Marías, J. (1987). *La felicidad humana*. Madrid: Alianza Editorial.

Marías, J. (1995). *Tratado de lo mejor: la moral y las formas de vida*. Madrid: Alianza Editorial.

Marías, J. (1999b). *La perspectiva cristiana*. Madrid: Alianza Editorial.

Marías, J. (1999a) 2000. *The Christian Perspective*. Trans. Harold Raley. Houston: Halcyon Press.

6

Julián Marías and Miguel de Unamuno on Christian Salvation and the Call for Personal Immortality

Abstract This chapter contrasts Julián Marías's and Miguel de Unamuno's positions with regard to Christian Salvation and the call for personal immortality. It is argued that although they should be considered as two distinct and independent philosophical positions, Marías's argumentation for justifying my (each one's) conscious hope for Christian Salvation through Resurrection bears some notable resemblances to Unamuno's reasoning in defence of his own notion of Christian religious faith that are relevant enough to make it reasonable to conclude that Marías formulated his argumentation in dialogue with Unamuno's position.

Keywords Christianity • Death • Immortality • Julián Marías • Miguel de Unamuno • Resurrection • Salvation

Miguel de Unamuno y Jugo (known as Miguel de Unamuno) was born on 29 September 1864 in Bilbao, in the Spanish region of the Basque Country, and died on 31 December 1936 in Salamanca, in the Spanish region of Castilla y León. Together with José Ortega y Gasset (1883–1955), Unamuno is generally accepted as the best-known and influential Spanish

© The Author(s), under exclusive license to Springer Nature Switzerland AG 2024
A. Oya, *The Metaphysical Anthropology of Julián Marías*, Palgrave Frontiers in Philosophy of Religion, https://doi.org/10.1007/978-3-031-61804-8_6

philosopher of the twentieth century, and the truth is that despite strictly speaking not forming a school of thought and having no disciples as such, his works had a profound influence on the philosophical and intellectual climate of twentieth century Spain.

In 1913, Unamuno published the essay *Del sentimiento trágico de la vida en los hombres y en los pueblos* (Unamuno 1913b) [*The Tragic Sense of Life in Men and Nations* (Unamuno 1913a)], which should be considered as his major philosophical work. In this book, Unamuno formulated a non-evidential notion of Christian religious faith while defending it in terms of its (alleged) natural foundation. Unamuno's religious faith consists in a non-evidentially grounded but still experientially felt religious understanding of the world, according to which the world ceases to appear as a mere "it" and is revealed to us as a personal loving Being who suffers as we do and who asks for our compassion and love. This religious understanding of the world moves us to the practice of charity—that is, to an agapeic way of conducting our own life and of relating to the whole world. It is through the practice of charity, through an agapeic giving ourselves over to the world, that the *feeling* of being in a loving communion with the whole world emerges in us, whereby we come to feel that our own singularity is increased without ceasing to be the same "men of flesh and bone" ("*hombres de carne y hueso*") we are here and now. Unamuno's religious faith emerges from what Unamuno named as the "tragic feeling of life" ("*sentimiento trágico de la vida*")—that is, the unresolvable struggle ("*agonía*") which, according to Unamuno, we all naturally and intimately felt between, on the one hand, our longing for the Christian God and His Salvation through Resurrection and, on the other hand, our incapacity to form the belief, on an evidential, rational basis, that the Christian God exists and that He is going to save us. Unamuno's faith is justified in terms of its natural foundation, inasmuch as the "tragic feeling of life" arises from what, according to Unamuno, is the most basic and natural inclination of all singular things, which is to increase their own singularity—named by Unamuno as the "hunger for immortality" ("*hambre de inmortalidad*"), since from this aiming at the increasement of our (each one's) singularity it follows, according to Unamuno, that we all seek for an endless existence.

Unamuno's notion of religious faith, and his argumentation in defence of it, is fully developed in his *Del sentimiento trágico de la vida en los hombres y en los pueblos.* However, its origins can be traced back to earlier papers such as "¡Pistis y no Gnosis!" (Unamuno 1897) ["¡Pistis and not Gnosis!"], "La fe" (Unamuno 1900b) ["Faith" (Unamuno 1900a)] and "Mi religión" (Unamuno 1907a) ["My religion" (Unamuno 1907a)]. Among his philosophical works, also worthy of mention is the essay *La agonía del cristianismo* (Unamuno 1924b) [*The Agony of Christianity* (Unamuno 1924a)], published in 1924 and mainly aimed at showing that the Christian conception of religious faith he had already defended in *Del sentimiento trágico de la vida en los hombres y en los pueblos* was not a proposal for a new understanding of Christianity, but amounted in fact to the original conception of religious faith defended by Early Christians and Jesus Christ.

In addition to his philosophical articles and essays, Unamuno published a large number of poems, plays and novels. In this regard, and despite Unamuno's philosophical reasoning already being clearly and systematically formulated in his *Del sentimiento trágico de la vida en los hombres y en los pueblos,* his literary works are still interesting when aiming to clarify his philosophical position. This is so because most of his literary works aim to *illustrate* in quotidian, non-philosophical technical jargon, the coherency of some of Unamuno's philosophical claims—let me emphasise, however, that Unamuno's novels are not, in any relevant sense, philosophical *argumentations* for such claims, inasmuch as they do not constitute conclusive logical arguments for the philosophical claims they aim to illustrate. The most well-known and obvious example in this regard is probably his short novel *San Manuel Bueno, mártir* (Unamuno 1930b) [*Saint Manuel Bueno, Martyr* (Unamuno 1930a)]. It is about the fictional character Manuel Bueno, a catholic priest from a small Spanish village who *because of* his incapacity to form the belief that the Christian God actually exists, and his consequent incapacity to believe that there is a personal existence after earthly death, he lovingly gives himself to the care of his people, for which he is sanctified by the church after his death. The novel aims to illustrate what is ultimately the core claim of Unamuno's conception of religious faith—that it is the lack of an evidential, rational justification for accepting the claim that God actually exists and that He is going to save us that moves us to a non-evidentially grounded but experientially felt religious understanding of the world, which in its turn leads us to an agapeic way of life, to the lovingly giving of oneself towards others and towards the world as a whole.[1]

Julián Marías (1914–2005) had no personal contact with Unamuno, apart from a brief encounter in the summer of 1934 during the *Universidad Internacional de Verano de Santander* ("International Summer University of Santander"), in which Unamuno and other intellectuals and professors were invited to take part, and which Marías attended as a student. However, Marías showed an early interest in the works of Unamuno, his first attempt at a coherent and systematic analysis of Unamuno's works occurring as early as 1938, when he was just 24 years old. On the New Year's Eve of 1938, exactly two years after Unamuno passed away and still in the midst of the Spanish Civil War (1936–1939), Marías finished his first essay on Unamuno, entitled "La obra de Unamuno: un problema de filosofía" (Marías 1938) ["The Work of Unamuno: A Problem of Philosophy"]. The essay was to be published in the journal *Hora de España*, which at the time was based in Barcelona, but at the end of January 1939 the Francoist troops took the city, leading to the journal being closed down and the issue in which Marías's essay was to appear never being published. Nonetheless, the upheavals of the war did not prevent Marías from pursuing his intention of offering an analysis of Unamuno's philosophy. Taking as a starting point his 1938 essay, Marías wrote his book entitled *Miguel de Unamuno* (Marías 1943b [Marías 1943a]). It was first published in 1943, and is one of the earlier, if not the earliest, serious monographic studies of Unamuno's works. The book was translated into English in 1966, proving influential both inside and outside Spain and establishing the basis for early scholarly discussions on Unamuno.

Marías's references to Unamuno did not end with this book, but he mentioned him in many of his writings thereafter, sufficing to show that Marías's interest in Unamuno was continuous and sincere and not simply a passing youthful whim. In 1998, when Marías was eighty-four years old

---

[1] For a detailed analysis of *San Manuel Bueno, mártir*, see my "Unamuno's Religious Faith in *San Manuel Bueno, mártir*" (Oya 2023a).

and sixty years after writing his first essay on Unamuno, he published a newspaper article entitled "La perduración de Unamuno" (Marías 1998) ["The Perdurance of Unamuno"]. In it, even when pointing out that Unamuno lacked of sufficient conceptual systematicity, Marías overtly recognises the philosophical relevance of his works, to the point of claiming that he is "unrenounceable":

> Among the thousands of articles he [Unamuno] wrote, a distinction must be made between those that sprang from within, out of a vital need, and those that meant something superficial, motivated by current events, by exasperation, sometimes by grumpiness, as sterile as ever. We must get to the bottom of Unamuno, to what he had to be, to what he expressed to live, to try to be who he was. Then one discovers that he is unrenounceable. His philosophical discoveries—"involuntary", if this word is understood, shunned, almost denied—are astonishing. It can be seen the extent to which he anticipated what was to be seen and later possessed, with resources he did not have, but which he felt with strange accuracy. It could be said that Unamuno "looked"—and, therefore, saw—what he did not know how to conceptualise and express adequately. (Marías 1998)[2]

In another of his newspaper articles, published in 1986 and entitled "La compañía de Unamuno" (Marías 1986) ["The Company of Unamuno"], Marías acknowledges his enthusiasm for Unamuno, even while certainly not agreeing with everything he said. Marías also acknowledges that his writings on Unamuno were guided by his commitment to convey and make accessible Unamuno's philosophical insights:

> My enthusiasm for Unamuno had been great since I began to read him in my early youth. I did not always agree with him, I was sometimes pained

---

[2] My translation. The original Spanish text reads: "Entre los millares de artículos que escribió, se impone una distinción entre los que brotaron desde dentro, por una necesidad vital, y los que significaron algo superficial, motivado por la actualidad, por la exasperación, en ocasiones por el malhumor, tan estéril como siempre. Hay que llegar al fondo de Unamuno, a lo que tuvo que ser, a lo que expresó para poder vivir, para intentar ser quien era. Entonces se descubre que es irrenunciable. Sus descubrimientos filosóficos, 'involuntarios', si se entiende esta palabra, rehuidos, casi negados, son asombrosos. Se ve hasta qué punto anticipó lo que había de verse y poseerse después, con recursos de que no disponía, pero que palpó con extraño acierto, Se diría que Unamuno 'miró' –y, por tanto, vio– lo que no supo conceptuar y expresar adecuadamente".

by his impulsiveness, his exaggeration, which led him to arbitrariness or injustice; but I admired his capacity for rectification, his tendency towards a final integration of external positions. Since he died, I have tried to ensure that his death was not irreparable. I endeavored, above all, to understand him, to save what was creative and veritable in him, to pass it on to others; I was determined that he should not be lost, that Spaniards should not be deprived of his fruitful action, that his figure should not be reduced to an abstract scheme or a caricature. (Marías 1986)[3]

In a scholarly essay published in 1982 and entitled "La pervivencia de Unamuno" (Marías 1982) ["The Survivance of Unamuno"], Marías similarly recognised the importance of Unamuno's legacy, going as far as to claim that Unamuno is an irreplaceable part of Spain:

[…] Unamuno survives as *part of Spain*. He is an ingredient, minimal in comparison with its total magnitude, but unmistakable, irreplaceable, unrenounceable, of the great living, historical, changing significance, waxing and waning like the moon, of the name "Spain". To say Spain in the twentieth century—and I think *since* the twentieth century—is to say, among other things, "Unamuno". This is what many, guessing it while he was alive, did not forgive him, what others do not forgive him, what fills some of us with joy. (Marías 1982, p. 27, author's emphasis)[4]

The aforementioned writings suffice to show that Marías's interest in Unamuno was not a youthful whim, but was persistent and lifelong. In addition to these writings, Marías wrote three essays that are interesting

---

[3] My translation. The original Spanish text reads: "Mi entusiasmo por Unamuno había sido grande, desde que empecé a leerlo, en mi primera juventud. No estaba siempre de acuerdo con él, me dolía a veces su embalamiento, su exageración, que lo llevaba a la arbitrariedad o la injusticia; pero admiraba su capacidad de rectificación, su tendencia a una integración final de posiciones externas. Desde que murió procuré que su muerte no fuera irreparable. Me esforcé, ante todo, por comprenderlo, por salvar lo que en él había de creador y verdadero, por transmitirlo a los demás; me propuse que no se perdiera, que los españoles no quedaran privados de su acción fecunda, que su figura no se redujera a un esquema abstracto o una caricatura".

[4] My translation. The original Spanish text reads: "[…] Unamuno pervive como *parte de España*. Es un ingrediente, mínimo en comparación con su magnitud total, pero inconfundible, insustituible, irrenunciable, de la gran significación viviente, histórica, cambiante, creciente o menguante, como la luna, del nombre 'España'. Decir España en el siglo XX –y creo que *desde* el siglo XX– es decir, entre otras cosas, 'Unamuno'. Esto es lo que muchos, por adivinarlo mientras vivía, no se lo perdonaban, lo que otros no le perdonan, lo que a algunos nos llena de alegría".

to mention here: "Lo que ha quedado de Miguel de Unamuno" (Marías 1954) ["What Has Remained of Miguel de Unamuno"], "La filosofía actual y el ateísmo" (Marías 1968b) ["Contemporary Philosophy and Atheism" (Marías 1968a)] and "La *'Meditatio Mortis'*, tema de nuestro tiempo" (Marías 1968d) ["*Meditatio Mortis'*—Theme of Our Time" (Marías 1968c)]. They are relevant in this regard because in them Marías explicitly points to Unamuno when making the claim that in the face of death my living (each one's) becomes a futile, impracticable task. As already explained in Chap. 4, this is a crucial premise of Marías's argumentation to conclude that *my life* (each one's) intrinsically postulates its own indefinite perdurance. In *Antropología metafísica: la estructura empírica de la vida humana* (Marías 1970b) [*Metaphysical Anthropology. The Empirical Structure of Human Life* (Marías 1970a)], the claim that faced with death living becomes an impracticable task is made with no explicit mention of Unamuno. Contrarily, and despite Marías not adhering to Unamuno's reasoning for claiming that we all seek for an endless existence, in all three of the essays just mentioned, Marías formulates this claim with explicit reference to Unamuno—see, for example, the following quote from "Lo que ha quedado de Miguel de Unamuno":

He [Unamuno] used to say that there is but one "single question"; to know if I am to die completely or not: "And if I do not die", he added, "what will become of me? And if I die, nothing has any sense anymore." Except for the congenital exaggeration that he attributed to the question of perdurance, I have to say that I completely agree, because I certainly believe that if we died completely, nothing would make sense anymore; and it would not make sense, of course, from now on, without waiting for us to die. (Marías 1954, p. 268; see also: Marías 1968a, p. 116 [Marías 1968b, p. 538] *and* Marías 1968c, pp. 124–125 [Marías 1968d, pp. 544–545])[5]

---

[5] My translation. The original Spanish text reads: "Solía decir que no hay más que una 'única cuestión'; saber si he de morir del todo, o no: 'Y si no muero –agregaba–, ¿qué será de mí? Y si muero, ya nada tiene sentido'. Salvo la congénita exageración que atribuía a la cuestión de la pervivencia, tengo que decir que estoy completamente de acuerdo, porque creo, efectivamente, que si muriésemos del todo, ya nada tendría sentido; y no lo tendría, por supuesto, desde ahora, sin esperar a que nos muriésemos".

The aim of this chapter is to contrast Marías's and Unamuno's positions with regard to Christian Salvation and the call for personal immortality. The comparison will show that although they should be considered as two distinct and independent positions which are therefore philosophically relevant on their own, they nonetheless bear some notable resemblances that are relevant enough to make it reasonable to conclude that Marías's argumentation for justifying my (each one's) conscious hope for Christian Salvation through Resurrection was formulated in dialogue with Unamuno's argumentation in defence of his own notion of Christian religious faith.

Let me begin with a brief overview of Unamuno's philosophical position. What follows is detailed enough to allow Marías's position to be contrasted, but is necessarily incomplete to ensure brevity. A much more detailed and systematic account of Unamuno's notion of Christian faith and his reasoning in defence of it can be found in my book *Unamuno's Religious Fictionalism* (Oya 2020a). The analysis I offered in that book was later complemented by several papers, the most relevant of which are: "Nietzsche and Unamuno on *Conatus* and the Agapeic Way of Life" (Oya 2020b), in which I show why Unamuno considered his notion of religious faith to be an exercise of self-affirmation, and why it can be considered as a convincing response to Nietzsche's criticisms of the Christian, agapeic way of life; "Unamuno and James on Religious Faith" (Oya 2020c), in which I show, against what seems to be the most common reading among Unamuno scholars, that Unamuno should not be considered as a pragmatist philosopher in any philosophical relevant sense of the term, and why his reasoning cannot be identified with William James's argument for religious belief as stated in his "The Will to Believe"; "Unamuno and the Makropulos Debate" (Oya 2022a), in which I argue that, despite what it may seem at first glance, Unamuno's claim that we all, without exception, suffer from what he named as "hunger for immortality" ("*hambre de inmortalidad*") is irrelevant for the contemporary philosophical debate on the *desirability* of enjoying an endless existence, the so-called Makropulos Debate; and "Unamuno on the Ontological Status of God and Other Fictional Characters" (Oya 2023b), in which I show that Unamuno conceived of God (and ordinary, non-religious fictional characters more generally) in realist though non-evidentially grounded terms, and that this way of conceiving of God allowed Unamuno to claim the actual existence of God (although as a fictional, purely humanly created character) and with it the possibility of there being an actual relationship between the concrete religious person and God—in "Religious Fictionalism and the Ontological Status of God" (Oya 2023b), I engage in the more general discussion, not explicitly framed in relation to Unamuno, about why a fictionalist understanding of God along the lines that Unamuno proposed, despite allowing the possibility of the religious person standing in an actual relation to God, fails to preserve a genuine *personal* relationship between the concrete religious person and God. If the reader is interested in a more detailed and systematic account of Unamuno's position than what follows, I humbly encourage them to read my aforementioned works.

The starting point of Unamuno's argumentation is his affirmation that the most basic and natural inclination of *all* singular things is to increase their own singularity. Unamuno refers to this (alleged) most basic and natural inclination as the "hunger for immortality" ("*hambre de inmortalidad*") since, according to Unamuno, from this aiming at the increasement of one's own singularity it follows that all singular things seek for an endless existence—which in our case, as human beings, means that we seek to endlessly continue to be the same "men of flesh and bone" ("*hombres de carne y hueso*") we already are here and now. Two crucial aspects regarding Unamuno's "hunger for immortality" should be emphasised. First, it is not a *desire* but a natural and primary inclination—that is, an *appetite* in Spinoza's jargon. Second, it refers to *all* singular things—that is, not only us human beings and complex animals but also *prima facie* non-sentient beings such as plants and rocks seek, primarily and naturally, to increase their own singularity. It is also interesting to point out that when defending this "hunger for immortality", Unamuno does not offer a novel argument of his own but rather relies on Spinoza's argument for the *conatus* as stated in the third part of the *Ethics* (Spinoza 1677, pp. 498–500).[6] However, and contrary to what Spinoza argues, Unamuno claims that what follows from Spinoza's argument is not a natural tendency towards self-preservation but a natural tendency towards the *increasement* of one's own singularity:

> The essence of a being is not only the endeavor to persist forever, as Spinoza taught us, but also the endeavor to become universal; it is a hunger and thirst for eternity and for infinity. Every created being tends not only to preserve itself in itself, but to perpetuate itself, and moreover, to encroach upon all else, to be all others without ceasing to be itself, to extend its limits to infinity, but yet without breaking them down. It does not wish to demolish its walls, and thus lay everything flat, communal, defenseless, confounding and losing its own identity, but wishes to push its walls to the extreme limits of creation and to encompass everything within them. It seeks the maximum of individuality with the maximum also of personality; it aspires to identify itself with the Universe, it aspires to God. (Unamuno 1913a, pp. 227–228 [Unamuno 1913b, p. 232])

Despite us all naturally (and so inevitably) seeking for an endless existence, all the evidence we have leads us to the conclusion that earthly death amounts to our annihilation (see, e.g., Unamuno 1913a, pp. 88–89 [Unamuno 1913b, p. 156]). Traditional philosophical arguments for the immortality of the soul fail in their purpose, according to Unamuno, because they are construed upon the unjustified assumption that

---

[6] Spinoza's argument for the *conatus* can be outlined as follows. The argument starts from the premise that "No thing can be destroyed except through an external cause" (Spinoza 1677, p. 498). Spinoza's defence of this premise consists in pointing out that a definition of a thing states the essence of that thing (i.e., that which makes the thing be the thing it is), and therefore that only something external to the definition of that thing can imply its destruction (i.e., its ceasing to be the thing it is). According to Spinoza, from this premise it follows that a thing is opposed to that which is contrary to its own nature: "Things are of a contrary nature, i.e., cannot be in the same subject, insofar as one can destroy the other" (Spinoza 1677, p. 498). If a thing were not opposed to that which is contrary to its own nature, it would be possible that that thing were to self-destruct (i.e., that that thing might contain in its very essence something that could make it cease to be the thing it is), but this is something impossible given the previous premise. From the conjunction of these two premises, Spinoza infers that all singular things have a non-teleological primary natural tendency towards self-preservation, which constitutes their most basic inclination: "Each thing, as far as it can by its own power, strives to persevere in its being" (Spinoza 1677, p. 498). This natural tendency Spinoza speaks about is now usually known by the term "*conatus*"—which was the original Latin word used by Spinoza and is now usually translated into English as "striving" or "seeking".

consciousness is a substance (Unamuno 1913a, pp. 93–96 [Unamuno 1913b, pp. 158–160]). Moreover, even conceding that these arguments could succeed in demonstrating that there are souls, substantial selves, that somehow survive after our earthly death, the conclusion we would be led to draw would still be that our most basic and natural inclination will not be satisfied. What we primarily and naturally seek for is continuing to be the same concrete individuals we already are here and now, and it is clear that what we are now is not fleshless, substantial souls but "men of flesh and bone". As Unamuno puts it:

> Without some kind of body or spirit-cover, the immortality of the pure soul is not true immortality. In the end, what we long for is a prolongation of this life, of this life and no other, this life of flesh and suffering, this life which we abominate at times precisely because it comes to an end. (Unamuno 1913a, p. 254 [Unamuno 1913b, p. 246])

We would therefore appear to be trapped in a contradictory situation. The conclusion that earthly death amounts to annihilation seems undeniable, but despite this we cannot stop seeking for an endless existence inasmuch as this seeking constitutes our most basic and natural inclination. This situation changes, Unamuno argues, once we become aware of the Biblical testimony about the Resurrection of Jesus Christ and His announcement of God's Salvation through Resurrection. Christian Salvation through Resurrection appears as the *only* kind of immortality we are aware of that claims to involve a kind of after earthly death existence that is fully personal, inasmuch as it refers to the continuing existence of us (each one of us) as the "men of flesh and bone" we are here and now. This led Unamuno to conclude that *only* if the Christian God were to exist and save us through Resurrection would our most basic and natural inclination to increase our own singularity, and so to enjoy of an endless existence, be fulfilled—"And there is only one name that satisfies our longing, and it is the name Saviour, Jesus" (Unamuno 1913a, p. 199 [Unamuno 1913b, p. 216]). Once we become aware of this, Unamuno argues, we cannot but come to *mediately* seek for the existence of the Christian God and His Salvation through Resurrection—mediately, but nonetheless inevitably, inasmuch as God's Salvation through Resurrection appears as the only means we are aware of by which our (each one's) most basic and natural inclination would be satisfied.

The question now, of course, is if we are justified in believing that God exists and that He is going to save us through Resurrection. Unfortunately, and according to Unamuno, this question cannot be solved on an evidential, rational basis. While there is no argument that succeeds in positively demonstrating the non-existence of God, arguments from natural theology fail in their purpose of demonstrating that God does exist. In brief, the problem with arguments from natural theology is that ultimately they are constructed as abductive inferences and therefore aim to justify the existence of God as being the best explanation for some given worldly event, but in so doing they end up converting God into nothing more than a scientific theoretical entity, an explanatory cause—and from this (alleged) explanatory causal role God's Salvation through Resurrection cannot be inferred (see: Unamuno 1913a, pp. 172–186 [Unamuno 1913b, pp. 201–209]).

Therefore, and despite our longing for God's Salvation, we cannot come to believe that God actually exists and that He is going to save us. This situation of ours is what Unamuno named as the "tragic feeling of life" ("*sentimiento trágico de la vida*")—that is, the struggle ("*agonía*") between, on the one hand, our longing for the Christian God and His Salvation through Resurrection, and on the other hand, our incapacity to form the belief, on an evidential, rational basis, that this God exists and that He is going to save us. This is not a theoretical conflict but a struggle that each of us intimately feels—which is why Unamuno named it "feeling" ("*sentimiento*").[7] Unamuno named it "tragic" ("*trágico*") because the struggle is unresolvable—as already explained, the question of the existence of God and whether He is going to save us through Resurrection cannot be solved on an evidential, rational basis, even though we cannot stop longing for this Salvation to occur inasmuch as it is the only means by which our most basic and natural inclination would be satisfied. The struggle is "of life" ("*de la vida*") because it does not emerge from any

---

[7] For no clear reason, Unamuno's "*sentimiento trágico de la vida*" is commonly translated into English as "tragic sense of life". However, the English equivalent for the Spanish word "*sentimiento*" is "feeling" and not "sense", the Spanish equivalent of which is "*sentido*". The correct English translation of "*sentimiento trágico de la vida*" is, therefore, "tragic feeling of life".

given trait of the world but from our own constitutive condition, as a reaction to what, according to Unamuno, is our (each one's) most basic and natural inclination—the "hunger for immortality".

The "tragic feeling of life" causes us a sort of anguish ("*congoja*"), and since the struggle is unresolvable, we cannot free ourselves from the anguish that goes with it—we can do nothing but commiserate with ourselves. As mentioned before, Unamuno's "hunger for immortality" refers not only to human beings but to all singular things. Therefore, each and all singular things without exception aim at the increasement of their own singularity, and so at endlessly continuing to be the same individuals they already are here and now, which means that not only us, human beings, but each and every singular thing suffers from the same miserable condition that we do. Once we become aware of this "universal woe" ("*miseria universal*"), we cannot but come to commiserate with each and every singular thing, and with the world as a whole (Unamuno 1913a, p. 229 [Unamuno 1913b, p. 233]). Only conscious, personal beings suffer, so claiming that the world as a whole suffers as we do is to conceive the world in a personal way. Moreover, commiserating presupposes love, given that we only commiserate with those to whom we somehow feel affectively related. Commiserating with the world is therefore loving the world—and to love the world is to conceive the world in a personal way, since we do not love things but persons. This is how, according to Unamuno, the world ceases to appears to us as a mere "it" and is revealed to us as a personal living Being, who suffers as we do and who asks for our compassion and love. In Unamuno's words:

> Spiritual love for oneself, the compassion one feels for oneself, may perhaps be called egotism, but nothing could be more opposed to common ordinary egotism. For from this love or compassion for yourself, from this intense despair, from the knowledge that just as before you were born you did not exist so after you die you will be no more, you go on to feel compassion for—that is, to love—all your fellow beings and brothers in this world of appearance, those wretched shadows who file by, going from nothingness to nothingness, mere sparks of consciousness shining for a moment in the infinite and eternal darkness. And from feeling compassion for other men, for those akin to you, beginning with those most akin to

you, for those you live among, you go on to feel compassion for everyone alive, and perhaps even for that which does not live but merely exists. That distant star shining up there in the night will one day be extinguished and turn to dust and cease shining and existing. And as with the one star, so it will be with the whole of the starry sky. Poor sky! [...] If I am moved to pity and love the luckless star which will one day vanish from the sky, it is because love, compassion, makes me feel that it possesses a consciousness, more or less obscure, which causes it to suffer because it is no more than a star doomed to cease being itself one day. For all consciousness is an awareness of death and suffering. [...] And when love is so great and vital, so strong and overflowing, that it loves everything, then it personalizes everything and discovers that the total Whole, the Universe, is also a Person with a Consciousness, a Consciousness which suffers, pities and loves, and is therefore consciousness. And this Consciousness of the Universe, which love discovers by personalizing whatever it loves, is what we call God. (Unamuno 1913a, pp. 152–154 [Unamuno 1913b, pp. 191–192])

This way of understanding the world moves us to the practice of charity—that is, to an agapeic way of conducting our own life and of relating to the whole world. Charity, our lovingly giving ourselves to the world, leads us *to feel as if we were* part of others, and of the world as a whole, and so to *feel* that our own singularity is increased without thereby ceasing to be the same "men of flesh and bone" that we are here and now (see: Unamuno 1913a, pp. 304–307 [Unamuno 1913b, pp. 274–275]).

It is crucial to emphasise that Unamuno's religious faith does not, and does not aim to, demonstrate the existence of God—and much less the claim that He will actually save us through Resurrection. The "tragic feeling of life" remains unresolvable no matter what we do. As previously explained, it is precisely as a reaction to the impossibility of resolving the struggle, and the anguish this impossibility brings with it, that Unamuno's religious faith emerges—meaning that if the question of the existence of (the Christian) God and His Salvation were to be conclusively resolved, either in the negative or in the positive, Unamuno's religious faith would simply not emerge. Neither the religious understanding of the world as a personal living Being who suffers as we do and who asks for our love and compassion that according to Unamuno we become immersed in after realising the "universal woe", nor the *feeling* of being in communion with the world as a whole that the practice of charity brings to us are, there-fore, evidence for claiming the actual existence of the Christian God. Unamuno's religious faith emerges as the subjective reaction to our (each one's) own constitutive condition and not to any given trait of the world—which is why it cannot amount to evidence regarding the world being such and such a way and not otherwise. This kind of non-evidentially grounded but still experientially felt religious understanding of the world that Unamuno's religious faith involves is akin to becoming immersed in a religious fiction, which is why Unamuno's religious faith can be considered as an earlier example of what philosophers nowadays tend to name as "religious fictionalism" (see: Oya 2020a, pp. 77–86).

This brief discussion of Unamuno's philosophy evinces that Marías's argumentation for justifying my (each one's) conscious hope for Christian Salvation through Resurrection cannot be identified with Unamuno's argumentation in defence of his own notion of religious faith. As the preceding chapters of this book have shown, in Marías's argumentation there is no reference to anguish nor to any sort of intimate struggle resem-bling Unamuno's "tragic feeling of life". They should therefore be consid-ered as two different and original philosophical positions on their own. However, even while Marías's argumentation cannot be identified with that of Unamuno, they still bear some notable resemblances that are wor-thy of comment.

First of all, and as previously mentioned, Unamuno's contention is to justify his own notion of Christian religious faith not because of it being grounded in the truth of some theological or religious statement, but rather because it is the outcome of what he claims to be my (each one's) ultimate constitutive condition—that is, the "hunger for immortality". Likewise, and as already explained in detail in Chaps. 4 and 5 of this book, Marías's contention is to justify my (each one's) conscious hope for Christian Salvation through Resurrection not because the certainty or at least the likelihood that such Salvation will, as a matter of fact, actually occur, but because it constitutes a conscious endorsement of my own *human* reality—inasmuch as only if this Salvation *were to occur* would the ontological postulate intrinsic to *my life* (each one's) referring to its own indefinite perdurance be fulfilled. Therefore, the first notable resemblance is that both argumentations aim to justify my (each one's) conscious endorsement of a religious stance as it being a self-affirming exercise, a conscious endorsement of what each author claims to be my (each one's) own ultimate constitutive reality, and so a sign of authenticity. Therefore, in neither case should justification be understood in relation to truth—neither Unamuno's nor Marías's argumentations presuppose or aim to demonstrate the truth (nor even the likelihood) of any theological or religious statement.

The second notable resemblance is that both argumentations are ultimately grounded in the claim that we all long for an endless existence. In this regard, it should also be emphasised that they both have the merit of defending a religious stance by relying on our longing not to die without thereby implying any sort of pragmatic wager. However, it should also be mentioned that although both authors agree that my (each one's) seeking for personal immortality is not a mere desire but an ontological determination intrinsic to my (each one's) own ultimate constitutive reality, they differ in their arguments for making this affirmation. As explained previously, when affirming that all singular things suffer from the "hunger for immortality", Unamuno exclusively relied on Spinoza's argument for the *conatus*—with the aforementioned amendment that what really follows from this argument is not a striving for self-preservation but a striving for increasing one's own singularity. Despite the fact that, as mentioned at the beginning of this chapter, in his earliest formulations Marías makes explicit reference to Unamuno when claiming that in the face of death living becomes an impracticable task, the truth is that Marías's argument in this regard has nothing to do with either Unamuno's "hunger for immortality" or Spinoza's argument for the *conatus*. Rather, Marías offers an original argument of his own for affirming that *my life* (each one's) intrinsically postulates its own indefinite perdurance, which as already explained in detail in Chap. 4 is ultimately grounded in his own conception of human happiness as the realisation of living.

The last notable resemblance is that in both cases the connection with religion, and more concretely with Christianity, relies on the claim that only if the Christian God were to exist and save us through Resurrection would this intrinsic longing of us to enjoy of an endless existence be satisfied. It is in this sense that, irrespective of their peculiarities, they should both be considered as Christian positions.

These resemblances, together with the fact that from youth Marías was a great connoisseur of Unamuno's works, seem to me to be reason enough to conclude that Marías's argumentation for justifying my (each one's) conscious hope for Christian Salvation through Resurrection was formulated in dialogue with Unamuno's position. By this I do not mean, however, that Marías's argumentation can be reduced to that of Unamuno—as already mentioned, and contrary to Unamuno, Marías does not rely on any sort of intimate struggle resembling Unamuno's "tragic feeling of life".

Moreover, and regardless of the differences and resemblances there may be between Marías and Unamuno, it should be recognised that Marías went much deeper than Unamuno did, in the sense that Marías did not avoid the task of addressing in a systematic and original way complex philosophical questions that are highly relevant when reflecting on death, immortality and the possibility of Christian Salvation. In Unamuno's texts, many of these questions are either not explicitly addressed or only formulated in an intuitive, non-systematic way. Regardless of whether we agree more with one author or the other, this is a philosophical merit for which Marías should be acknowledged. For example, nowhere in Unamuno's texts is there an argument for showing that earthly death does not necessarily imply our complete personal annihilation—aside from the reference to the biblical testimony on the Resurrection of Jesus Christ, but neither is there any philosophical discussion about whether such an event might at least be conceptually possible. Likewise, and despite Unamuno's insistence that we are all irremediably going to die, he offers no argument for claiming the *necessity* of death. As already explained in the preceding chapters of this book, and in contrast to Unamuno, Marías explicitly addresses these and other related questions on the basis of his Metaphysical Anthropology. Ultimately, the problem is that despite Unamuno being clear that what we are is "men of flesh and bone", and even when at an intuitive level it is clear what he meant by that, he did not develop this claim into a systematic account of personal identity—and without a systematic account of personal identity, Unamuno could not provide a clear, straightforward answer to the questions that arise when discussing *personal* immortality. On the contrary, Marías's Metaphysical Anthropology involves a systematic characterisation of *man*, and *human life* more generally, which admittedly is much more developed and philosophically interesting than simply affirming that what we are is "men of flesh and bone", and that provides Marías with the necessary philosophical background to formulate his position in a much more systematic and rigorous way than did Unamuno.

In summary, there are some notable resemblances that make it reasonable to conclude that Marías's argumentation for justifying my (each one's) conscious hope for Christian Salvation through Resurrection was formulated in dialogue with Unamuno's argumentation in defence of his own notion of Christian religious faith. However, Marías's argumentation cannot be identified with that of Unamuno. Marías's and Unamuno's are therefore two different and original positions of their own—and, let me emphasise, they are philosophically relevant both in their own way and in their own right.

References

Marías, J. (1938) 1960. La obra de Unamuno: un problema de filosofía. In *Julián Marías: Obras (vol. V)*, 277–307. Madrid: Revista de Occidente.

Marías, J. (1943a) 1966. *Miguel de Unamuno*. Trans. Frances M. López-Morillas. Cambridge, Massachusetts: Harvard University Press.

Marías, J. (1943b) 1960. Miguel de Unamuno. In *Julián Marías: Obras (vol. V)*, 1–201. Madrid: Revista de Occidente.

Marías, J. (1954) 1960. Lo que ha quedado de Miguel de Unamuno. In *Julián Marías: Obras (vol. V)*, 263–276. Madrid: Revista de Occidente.

Marías, J. (1968a) 1971. Contemporary Philosophy and Atheism. In *Philosophy as Dramatic Theory*, trans. James Parsons, 91–113. Pennsylvania: The Pennsylvania State University Press.

Marías, J. (1968b) 1970. La filosofía actual y el ateísmo. In *Julián Marías: Obras (vol. VIII)*, 520–538. Madrid: Revista de Occidente.

Marías, J. (1968c) 1971. '*Meditatio Mortis*'—Theme of Our Time. In *Philosophy as Dramatic Theory*, trans. James Parsons, 117–130. Pennsylvania: The Pennsylvania State University Press.

Marías, J. (1968d) 1970. La '*meditatio mortis*', tema de nuestro tiempo. In *Julián Marías: Obras (vol. VIII)*, 539–548. Madrid: Revista de Occidente.

Marías, J. (1970a) 1971. *Metaphysical Anthropology: The Empirical Structure of Human Life.* Trans. Frances M. López-Morillas. Pennsylvania: The Pennsylvania State University Press.

Marías, J. (1970b). *Antropología metafísica: la estructura empírica de la vida humana.* Madrid: Revista de Occidente.

Marías, J. (1982) 1986. La pervivencia de Unamuno. *Cuenta y razón* 25: 9–27.

Marías, J. (1986). La compañía de Unamuno. *La Vanguardia* [Barcelona], 29 December 1986, p. 5.

Marías, J. (1998). La perduración de Unamuno. *ABC* [Madrid], 9 July 1998, p. 3.

Oya, A. (2020a). *Unamuno's Religious Fictionalism.* Cham: Palgrave Macmillan.

Oya, A. (2020b). "Nietzsche and Unamuno on *Conatus* and the Agapeic Way of Life". *Metaphilosophy* 51 (2–3): 303–317 [Reprinted in *Philosophy as a Way of Life: Historical, Contemporary, and Pedagogical Perspectives* (2020), eds. James M. Ambury, Tushar Irani, Kathleen Wallace, 141–154. Hoboken: Wiley.]

Oya, A. (2020c). Unamuno and James on Religious Faith. *Teorema. Revista Internacional de Filosofía* 39 (1): 85–104.

Oya, A. (2022a). Unamuno and the Makropulos Debate. *International Journal for Philosophy of Religion* 91: 111–114.

Oya, A. (2022b). Unamuno on the Ontological Status of God and Other Fictional Characters. *Teorema. Revista Internacional de Filosofía* 41 (3): 25–45.

Oya, A. (2023a). Unamuno's Religious Faith in *San Manuel Bueno, mártir*. In *Essays on Values—Volume 3*, eds. M. J. M. Branco and J. Constâncio, 383–410. Instituto de Filosofia da Nova (IFILNOVA).

Oya, A. (2023b). Religious Fictionalism and the Ontological Status of God. *Teorema. Revista Internacional de Filosofía* 42 (2): 133–151.

Spinoza, B. (1677) 1985. Ethics: Demonstrated in Geometrical Order and Divided into Five Parts. In *The Collected Works of Spinoza*, ed. and trans. E. M. Curley, 408–617. Princeton: Princeton University Press.

Unamuno, M. (1897) 1968. ¡Pistis y no Gnosis!. In *Miguel de Unamuno: obras completas (vol. III: 'Nuevos ensayos')*, ed. Manuel García Blanco, 681–685. Madrid: Escelier.

Unamuno, M. (1900a) 1974. Faith. In *The Selected Works of Miguel de Unamuno (vol. 5)*, ed. and trans. Anthony Kerrigan, 148–164. Princeton: Princeton University Press.

Unamuno, M. (1900b) 1966. La fe. In *Miguel de Unamuno: obras completas (vol. I: 'Paisajes y ensayos')*, ed. Manuel García Blanco, pp. 962–970. Madrid: Escelicer.

Unamuno, M. (1907a) 1966. My Religion. In *The Selected Works of Miguel de Unamuno (vol. 5)*, ed. and trans. Anthony Kerrigan, 209–217. Princeton: Princeton University Press.

Unamuno, M. (1907b) 1968. Mi religión. In *Miguel de Unamuno: obras completas (vol. III: "Nuevos ensayos")*, ed. Manuel García Blanco, 259–263. Madrid: Escelicer.

Unamuno, M. (1913a) 1972. The Tragic Sense of Life in Men and Nations. In *The Selected Works of Miguel de Unamuno (vol. 4)*, ed. and trans. Anthony Kerrigan, 3–358. Princeton: Princeton University Press.

Unamuno, M. (1913b) 1966. Del sentimiento trágico de la vida en los hombres y en los pueblos. In *Miguel de Unamuno: obras completas (vol. VII: 'Meditaciones y ensayos espirituales')*, ed. Manuel García Blanco, 109–302. Madrid: Escelicer.

Unamuno, M. (1924a) 1974. The Agony of Christianity. In *The Selected Works of Miguel de Unamuno (vol. 5)*, ed. and trans. Anthony Kerrigan, 1–109. Princeton: Princeton University Press.

Unamuno, M. (1924b) 1966. La agonía del cristianismo. In *Miguel de Unamuno: obras completas (vol. VII: 'Meditaciones y ensayos espirituales')*, ed. Manuel García Blanco, 303–364. Madrid: Escelicer.

Unamuno, M. (1930a) 1976. Saint Manuel Bueno, Martyr. In *The Selected Works of Miguel de Unamuno (vol. 7)*, ed. and trans. Anthony Kerrigan, 135–180. Princeton: Princeton University Press.

Unamuno. M. (1930b) 1967. San Manuel Bueno, mártir. In *Miguel de Unamuno: obras completas (vol. II: 'Novelas')*, ed. Manuel García Blanco, 1127–1154. Madrid: Escelicer.

7

Conclusion

Abstract This concluding chapter overviews the analysis offered in the previous chapters. Without thereby detracting from the philosophical relevance that the different argumentative steps that compose Marías's argumentation may have individually, it is stated that the ultimate relevance of Marías's proposal is to offer a way to justify my (each one's) conscious hope for Christian Salvation through Resurrection, and with it my hope for Christian Revelation to be true, by appealing to my (each one's) *human* reality and on the grounds of its hypothetical possibility, and with no intention of demonstrating, precisely because it is indemonstrable, either the truth or the likelihood that this Salvation will actually occur.

Keywords Christianity • Hope • Jesus Christ • Julián Marías • Metaphysical Anthropology • Personal immortality • Resurrection • Revelation • Salvation • Summary

This book provides a detailed account of Julián Marías's Metaphysical Anthropology, with the ultimate aim of offering a coherent and

© The Author(s), under exclusive license to Springer Nature Switzerland AG 2024
A. Oya, *The Metaphysical Anthropology of Julián Marías*, Palgrave Frontiers in Philosophy of Religion, https://doi.org/10.1007/978-3-031-61804-8_7

systematic analysis of Marías's argumentation for claiming that my (each one's) conscious hope for Christian Salvation through Resurrection—and with it my hope that Jesus Christ did actually resurrect, and more generally my hope for Christian Revelation to be true—is justified not because I am justified in affirming the truth or the likelihood that this Salvation will actually occur, but because this hope of mine is a legitimate reaction on my part, inasmuch as it amounts to a self-affirming exercise, a conscious endorsement of my own (each one's) *human* reality, and as such a sign of authenticity. As the preceding chapters of this book show, Marías's argumentation is complex, consisting of several argumentative steps. By way of conclusion, and leaving aside the first introductory chapter, this last chapter overviews the analysis offered in this book.

Chapter 2 is a biographical introduction to Julián Marías (1914–2005). An outline of Marías's life is given, and his most well-known essays and philosophical works are pointed out. This chapter indirectly provides an overview of the political situation of twentieth-century Spain—inasmuch as Marías's life was deeply interwoven with the two major political events in Spain's recent history: the Spanish Civil War (1936–1939) and the regime change that took place around 1975–1979, which saw Spain progress from the Francoist dictatorship to the consolidation of a democratic parliamentary system in the form of a constitutional monarchy, a period commonly referred to in Spain as "*la transición*" ("the Transition"). Marías's collaboration with the Republican side during the Spanish Civil War is commented on, helping to understand why his exclusion from the official intellectual institutions of the Francoist regime, which prevented him from obtaining a faculty position in Spain for the entire duration of the dictatorship, including from the 1950s onwards when his works were having a significant international impact and he was regularly being invited to lecture at American universities. Marías's relationship with José Ortega y Gasset (1883–1955), first as a university student and later as a disciple and friend, is pointed out, as is Marías's self-inclusion in the so-called *Escuela de Madrid* ("School of Madrid"), which includes thinkers such as Manuel García Morente (1886–1942), Xavier Zubiri (1898–1983) and José Gaos (1900–1969). Last, Marías's participation in the discussions on and approval of the Spanish Constitution of 1978 in his role as a senator during the so-called *legislatura constituyente* ("constituent legislature") is commented on.

Chapter 3 offers a detailed account of Marías's Metaphysical Anthropology, which expands in an innovative and philosophically relevant way on José Ortega y Gasset's ontological claim that *my life* (each one's) is the *radical reality* ("*realidad radical*"). Chapter 3 is divided into two sections. In the first section, Ortega's argument for claiming that *my life* (each one's) is the *radical reality* is analysed. To the classic controversy between naive realism, which claims that the world is a reality subsistent in itself and so is entirely independent of the concrete subject, and idealism, which claims that the conscience, the thinking I, is the primary reality, Ortega responded by arguing that the primary and fundamental reality is neither the world nor the I, but the coexistence between the world and the I—a claim which is schematically summarised in Ortega's formula "*Yo soy yo y mi circunstancia, y si no la salvo a ella no me salvo yo*" ("I am myself and my circumstance, and if I do not save it I do not save myself"). The second section contains a detailed account of Marías's Metaphysical Anthropology. The subject matter of Marías's Metaphysical Anthropology is the study of the realisation of *human life* in the form of *man*. Marías named his position as Metaphysical Anthropology because the apprehension of the determinations that are constitutive of the realisation of *human life* in the form of *man*—the concretisation of what Marías named as the *empirical structure of human life* ("*estructura empírica de la vida humana*"), and whose knowledge is obtained empirically—presupposes apprehension of the necessary conditions without which there is no *human life*—what Marías named as the *analytical structure of human life* ("*estructura analítica de la vida humana*"), and whose knowledge is obtained through metaphysical analysis of *my life*.

Chapter 4 discusses Marías's argumentation for concluding that my (each one's) conscious hope for personal immortality after my *biological death* occurs is justified inasmuch as it is a self-affirming exercise, a conscious endorsement of my own *human* reality, and so a sign of authenticity. This conclusion is grounded in Marías's claim that *my life* (each one's) presupposes, not as an epistemic attitude of part of I myself, the executive I, but as an ontological postulate intrinsic to *my life* without which *my life* itself as *radical reality* is *impossible*, the assumption of its own indefinite perduration. The different argumentative steps that compose Marías's argumentation in this regard are examined, including his conception of human happiness as the fulfilment of the task of living, his argument for claiming that *biological death* is an *anthropologically* necessary fact, his conceptual distinction between *biological death* and *personal death*, and his claim that corporeality is an *installation* pertaining to the *empirical structure of human life* as we find it realised in the reality *man*. Marías's argumentation ultimately consists in converting the *practical need* of presupposing one's own indefinite perdurance to face the futility of living given our inexorable certainty about the *anthropological* necessity of *biological death* into an *ontological postulate* referring to the indefinite perdurance of *my life* (each one's) without which *my life* as *radical reality* is itself *impossible*—as is therefore all reality inasmuch as, under Marías's premises, any reality must be *radicated* in *my life*. It is shown that the crucial step in Marías's argumentation is his identification of human happiness with the realisation of living. It is argued that this identification is problematic even under Marías's premises. Marías's identification of human happiness with the realisation of living implies that human happiness is a necessary installation of any *human life* regardless of its realisation on this or that concrete *empirical structure of human life*, and as such pertains to the *analytical structure of human life* as a necessary requisite without which there is no *human life*. However, the identification of human happiness with the realisation of living is not an analytical claim inferred from the metaphysical analysis of *my life,* but an empirical one exclusively grounded in my own empirical observation regarding the results of my living. Under the premises of Marías's Metaphysical Anthropology, this means that there is still the possibility of there being a *human life* distinct from *man* that may be realised on a different *empirical structure* which lacks of the installation of human happiness—so that, contrary to Marías's contention, human happiness cannot be identified with the realisation of living.

Chapter 5 analyses Marías's argumentation for concluding that my (each one's) conscious hope for Christian Salvation through Resurrection is justified as it being a conscious endorsement of my own *human* reality. The analysis shows that Marías's argumentation ultimately relies on the claim that only if the Christian God were to exist and save us through

Resurrection would the ontological postulate intrinsic to *my life* (each one's) regarding its own indefinite perduration then be satisfied. As Marías rightly points out, the real or factual possibility that Christian Salvation through Resurrection could actually occur lacks of philosophical justification since it is exclusively grounded in Christian Revelation—and more concretely in the hypothetical possibility that Jesus Christ did, as a matter of fact, actually resurrect. However, and according to Marías, there is no philosophical reason for denying that Christian Resurrection is conceptually possible. Moreover, neither does the way of conceiving personal reality involved in Christian Revelation contradict any philosophical claim—at least not those involved in Marías's Metaphysical Anthropology. In fact, they generally seem to coincide. There are, therefore, and according to Marías, no philosophical reasons contravening my (each one's) conscious hope for Christian Salvation through Resurrection—hence my (each one's) conscious hope for Christian Salvation through Resurrection remains justified as it being a conscious endorsement of my own ultimate *human* reality, inasmuch as only if this Salvation were to occur would the ontological postulate intrinsic to *my life* (each one's) regarding its own indefinite perdurance be satisfied. Although Marías does not seem to explicitly formulate this line of reasoning, it is argued that his argumentation offers a way to justify my (each one's) hope that Christian Revelation is true without thereby having to affirm its being true—since it is not possible to hope for Christian Salvation through Resurrection without also hoping that Christian Revelation is true, if my hope for Christian Salvation through Resurrection is justified, then my hope for Christian Revelation to be true is in principle also justified. It is argued that Marías's argumentation involves an argumentative transition from the premises of his Metaphysical Anthropology to the religious interpretation of Christian Revelation—and it is argued that this transition is unproblematic, both from a philosophical point of view and from a Christian point of view.

Chapter 6 helps to situate Marías within the framework of the history of Spanish Philosophy by contrasting his position with that of Miguel de Unamuno (1864–1936). The contrast shows that they are two different and original philosophical positions in their own right. However, while Marías's argumentation cannot be identified with that of Unamuno, it is argued that they bear some resemblances that make it reasonable to conclude that Marías formulated his own position in dialogue with Unamuno. These resemblances are three. First, both argumentations aim to justify my (each one's) conscious endorsement of a religious stance as it being a self-affirming exercise, a conscious endorsement of what each of these authors claim to be my own (each one's) ultimate constitutive reality, and so also a sign of authenticity. This is why in neither Unamuno's nor Marías's argumentations should justification be understood in relation to truth—none of their argumentations presuppose nor aim to demonstrate the truth (and not even the likelihood) of any theological or religious statement, but rather their focus is on the concrete subject and what emerges from him. Second, both argumentations are ultimately grounded in the claim that we all long for an endless existence and that this longing is not a mere desire but an ontological determination intrinsic to my (each one's) ultimate constitutive reality—although it should be noted that Marías and Unamuno differ in their arguments for making such an affirmation. Third, in both cases the connection with religion, and more concretely with Christianity, is grounded in the claim that only if Christian Salvation through Resurrection were to occur would the intrinsic longing of us to enjoy of an endless existence then be satisfied. These resemblances show one of the merits shared by both Unamuno and Marías, which is the ability to formulate a coherent defence of a Christian stance through appealing to our longing not to die, without thereby having to assume or demonstrate the truth that God actually exists and that He will bless us with an endless existence, and without relying on any sort of pragmatic wager. Last, it is argued that regardless of the resemblances and differences there may be between Marías's and Unamuno's positions, and regardless of which of them we agree with more, Marías's philosophical merit should be acknowledged in that he addresses in a systematic and original way complex philosophical questions that are highly relevant when reflecting on death, immortality and Christian Salvation, and that, in Unamuno's texts, are mostly either not explicitly addressed or remain formulated in a non-systematic, intuitive way.

As this book shows, Marías's argumentation is complex, involving several argumentative steps, most of which are innovative and philosophically relevant in their own right. Regardless of the philosophical relevance that these argumentative steps may have individually, the ultimate relevance of Marías's proposal is that it offers a way to justify my (each one's) conscious hope for Christian Salvation through Resurrection, and with it my hope for Christian Revelation to be true, by appealing to my (each one's) *human* reality and on the grounds of its hypothetical possibility, and with no intention of demonstrating, precisely because it is indemonstrable, either the truth or the likelihood that this Salvation will actually occur—indemonstrable because the possibility that Christian Salvation through Resurrection could actually occur is exclusively founded on the hypothetical possibility that Jesus Christ did actually resurrect, which is a *fact* that is seen and not a philosophical premise to be demonstrated through philosophical reasoning. From a philosophical point of view, this is a virtue of Marías's argumentation because it respects the boundaries of philosophical reasoning—it does not require philosophy to demonstrate what it cannot demonstrate. From a Christian point of view, this is a virtue inasmuch as it succeeds in preserving the foundational role of the Biblical testimony about the Resurrection of Jesus Christ together with its revealed, and so indemonstrable, character.

Index[1]

---

[1] Note: Page numbers followed by 'n' refer to notes.

© The Author(s), under exclusive license to Springer Nature Switzerland AG 2024
A. Oya, *The Metaphysical Anthropology of Julián Marías*, Palgrave Frontiers in
Philosophy of Religion, https://doi.org/10.1007/978-3-031-61804-8

SPRINGER NATURE

GPSR Compliance

The European Union's (EU) General Product Safety Regulation (GPSR) is a set of rules that requires consumer products to be safe and our obligations to ensure this.

If you have any concerns about our products, you can contact us on ProductSafety@springernature.com

In case Publisher is established outside the EU, the EU authorized representative is:

Springer Nature Customer Service Center GmbH
Europaplatz 3
69115 Heidelberg, Germany

The manufacturer's authorised representative in the EU is Springer
Nature Customer Service Centre GmbH, Europaplatz 3, 69115 Heidelberg,
Germany. If you have any concerns regarding our products, please
contact ProductSafety@springernature.com

Printed and bound by CPI Group (UK) Ltd, Croydon, CR0 4YY

29/04/2026

02099525-0007